BURPEE AMERICAN GARDENING SERIES

VEGETABLES

AMERICAN GARDENING SERIES

VEGETABLES

Suzanne Frutig Bales

PRENTICE
HALL
PRESS

New York ◆ London ◆ Toronto ◆ Sydney ◆ Tokyo ◆ Singapore

This book is dedicated to my father, Edward C. Frutig, whose help and encouragement made it possible.

PRENTICE HALL PRESS
15 Columbus Circle
New York, NY 10023

PRENTICE HALL PRESS and colophon are registered
trademarks of Simon & Schuster, Inc.

Library of Congress Cataloging in Publication Data

Bales, Suzanne Frutig.
    The Burpee American gardening series. Vegetables / Suzanne Frutig Bales.
       p.   cm.
    ISBN 0-13-093337-6 : $7.95
    1. Vegetable gardening.   2. Vegetables.   3. Vegetables—Pictorial
works.   I. Title.   II. Title: Vegetables.
SB321.B245   1991
635—dc20   90-34676
                                       CIP

Designed by Patricia Fabricant
Manufactured in the United States of America

First Edition January 1991

Burpee is a registered trademark of W. Atlee Burpee & Company.

PHOTOGRAPHY CREDITS
Agricultural Research Service, USDA
Alf Christianson Seed Co.
Bales, Suzanne Frutig
Dibblee, Steven
Druse, Ken
Fell, Derek
Known-You Seed Co., Inc.
Nourse Farms, Inc.
Petoseed Company, Inc.
Sakata Seed America, Inc.

Drawings by Michael Gale
Best Vegetable Garden watercolor by Jean LaRue
Best Vegetable Garden plan by Richard Gambier

I am happy to finally express my deep gratitude to the many people who have helped me while I was writing this book. My thanks go to Gina Norgard, Martha Kraska and my husband and partner, Carter F. Bales, for providing me with unending help, support and love and to Alice R. Ireys, my close friend and mentor.

I am indebted to horticulturists Chela Kleiber, Eileen Kearney, Steve Frowine, Carol Whitenack, Charles Cresson, Jim Hoge and Ralph Borchard; to the Burpee breeders Dr. Dennis Flaschenreim, Teresa Jacobsen, John J. Mondry, Dr. Nung Che Chen, Dr. Michael Burke and Lois Stringer; to Jonathan Burpee and the Burpee customer service department; and to photography coordinator Barbara Wolverton and administrative assistant Elda Malgieri.

At Prentice Hall Press I would like to thank Anne Zeman, publisher, editor and gardener, whose watchful eye, patience, enthusiasm and belief in these books have made them a reality; Rebecca Atwater, whose twist of a phrase and change of a word have greatly improved and polished these books; Rachel Simon for her patience and thoroughness.

Suzanne Frutig Bales

Cover: The abundance of harvest lasts for many months with a well-planned and maintained garden.

Preceding pages: Vegetables, herbs, and flowers for cutting grow side by side in the author's vegetable garden.

Last year was "potato parade." Potatoes have always been my favorite vegetable but I hadn't grown them, mistakenly believing they would take too much room in my garden and that the ones from the store were as tasty as home-grown. Was I mistaken! There are even more varieties, shapes, and colors of potatoes than of tomatoes, from long, purple fingers to small, round, solid blue, red, and yellow. For inclusion in the vegetable garden, potatoes have moved right to the top of my list, next to tomatoes.

The purpose of this book, as well as of the others in the "Burpee American Gardening Series," is to spread the pleasure that comes from gardening, and to help and encourage new gardeners. It also aims to challenge more experienced gardeners to try less familiar plants and new ideas, while sharing the knowledge Burpee seedsmen have accumulated over one hundred years of breeding, growing, and harvesting seeds.

At Burpee we concentrate on a practical approach, giving the gardener choices that will accommodate a busy lifestyle. Here we believe everyone can benefit from gardening, feeling closer to nature and the changing seasons, and taking pride in the bounty of the harvest.

The joys of gardening are great, and the sorrows and disappointments few. Like anything worthwhile, good gardening takes practice, patience, and, to start, a little knowledge. But it's so rewarding! Nothing tastes like fresh-picked, garden-grown, home-cooked vegetables—except fresh-picked, garden-grown, home-cooked vegetables.

When next year's catalogs arrive, I will again scheme and plan my garden. So many choices, so little room, and so much fun. We hope that in the pages that follow, you will find at least one thought or suggestion that will help you celebrate the wonder of gardening.

PLANNING

I think the main reason I grow vegetables stems from happy childhood memories, of sitting on the back steps at the end of summer, slurping a freshly picked, sun-warmed tomato, the juice tickling and pouring down my chin. Unbeatable flavor straight from the garden. As a child, I enjoyed only the harvest. As an adult, I love the exercise and good health that come from working in a garden. It's rewarding to watch the changing, ripening fruit and, later, to share the harvest with friends and neighbors. Over the years I became increasingly aware of the harmful pesticides used on commercially grown vegetables. I like knowing that my home-grown vegetables are safe and nutritious for my children. These are some of my reasons for growing a vegetable garden.

It is important for you to examine your reasons for growing a vegetable garden. There are many sorts of vegetable garden, and what sort you choose should depend on what you hope to achieve. A vegetable garden takes more planning than any other form of garden. Vegetables need more from the soil than other plants, so you must prepare it properly.

Not only must the soil be brought to as nutritious a condition as possible, but the plan for the growing season could include intensive planting, too (using the same soil for more than one crop). You will want a soil rich enough at all times to bring a full measure of vitamins, nutrients and flavor to your crop and, finally, to your table.

1
THE VEGETABLE GARDEN PLANNER

Vegetable gardening is for the adventuresome, imaginative child in each of us. It's never dull.

My vegetable garden changes constantly, seemingly by happenstance. Sometimes I select plant varieties on a whim, and the garden changes direction with the breeze: Each year I add to the staples I'm sure we can't be without. I've learned there are more interesting, unusual, and rewarding plants than can be grown in a lifetime. The best advice for the beginning gardener is to follow your instincts, try new vegetables, let yourself be challenged, experiment! If you like to cook, you are luckier still. The opportunities with new vegetables are limitless.

The Chinese remember the years with the names of animals—the year of the monkey, the year of the dragon, and so forth. I remember my summers by the vegetables that held my enthusiasm: the summer of the Chinese vegetables, the tomato medley, the potato parade, and the vine teepees, to name just a few. By indulging my interests, I've been rewarded with wonderful memories, an education, an expanded palate, and more vegetables to add to the list of "favorites," vegetables I refuse to go without each summer.

Looking back over the last few years, the summer of the Chinese vegetables stands out as the most unusual, with bitter melon, fuzzy melon, and cucuzzi tucked in among the more conventional Chinese vegetables of snow peas, pak choi and Chinese cabbage. The cucuzzi was especially beguiling. It made an acceptable soup, but it wasn't as delicious as it was simply fascinating, a fast-growing, vining squash with long, narrow S-shaped fruits that reached four to five feet. The vines grew over the fence, into the roses, and out again across the lawn 20 feet or more to the walk. We just let it grow. It was harmless enough, a great conversation piece, strange and wonderful to watch. Once, I spied the kids fencing with the largest of the fruits. We grow cucuzzi every year now, to instill in our children respect for the miracle of growth. The cucuzzi demands attention; it is impossible to avoid just watching it grow.

The summer of the tomato medley was tame by comparison. Until then, I had grown only red tomatoes, never yellow or pink. The sizes, shapes, and colors available were an education in themselves: small fruits to whoppers, in pear and ball shapes, in shades of yellow, red, and pink. It was very interesting to serve them to guests. Even though the yellow tomatoes seem milder—and seem to taste less acid—some people shy away because of the unfamiliar color. In my blindfold test, the yellow tomatoes were noticeably milder—a big winner.

One truth manifests itself every year: No matter how carefully I plan what to plant, I never have enough tomatoes and always have too many zucchini. (In Vermont, summer wisdom dictates that you always lock your car at the shopping mall or some generous soul will come along and fill it with zucchini.) I happen to love zucchini every which way: in soup and bread, stuffed and sautéed . . . you name it. Zucchini is kind to the beginning gardener because it almost never disappoints, but be aware that it is a very prolific plant.

Our "Indian" summer featured peas and beans grown on tall poles tied together into teepees the children played in. The floor of each teepee was carpeted with black plastic and covered with mounds of salt hay to fluff like pillows.

One of the pleasures of vegetable gardens is harvesting.

CONTENTS

When planning a vegetable garden, the first decision is to choose a site for the garden. It should be fairly level, but not at the bottom of an incline where water will stand in puddles after a heavy rain. Be sure it's away from any tree or shrub roots, which compete for space and nutrients in the soil (to say nothing of the unwanted shade the foliage of the plant may provide). Vegetable crops need light and warmth from the sun, and the spot you choose must provide at least six hours of direct sun per day. The more sun, the better; for a vegetable garden, full-sun locations are best.

Beginners should think small. A 10-foot-by-10-foot garden will be very productive without being a burden. There is a lot to learn and to remember in your first garden. Gardening, like riding a bike, seems difficult to the beginner but is a cinch once you get the hang of it.

Start with a diagram of the garden; it needn't be accurate to the inch. Use graph paper and a scale of ¼ inch to the foot for easy reading. The purpose of a diagram is twofold. First, when you plan what you grow this year and in what location, you'll know what quantities to plant; second, you'll know which crops to locate next to each other. Your notebook will remind you next year on the position of crops in the garden, when they were planted, when seedlings first appeared, and when you harvested. Keeping a record will help you learn when to pick the early crops and when you can follow with the second planting. You can plan ahead and start the seeds indoors so the seedlings are ready as garden space becomes available.

It is important to rotate crops from year to year. This helps avoid soil and insect problems that result from repeated planting of the same crops in the same areas. "Rotating" means only that you do not grow the same plant in exactly the same spot two years in succession. For proper crop rotation, you need move plants only a few feet away from their previous location.

CHECKLIST FOR PLANNING A VEGETABLE GARDEN

1. Plant the tallest-growing vegetables at the north end of the vegetable garden, so they don't shade the shorter plants.
2. Rotate vegetables every year.
3. Check spacing requirements for the recommended distance between rows. Close spacing leaves little room for weeds, but more space is needed to accommodate the use of a mechanical cultivator. Give the roots all the room they need to grow.
4. Plan paths for walking and working in the garden. Will you want to bring a wheelbarrow into the garden? If so, paths should be three feet wide. Leave comfortable working room.
5. Group long-season crops together for ease in preparing the soil. The bed will need to be prepared only once; it can be mulched, the crop harvested, and finally plowed under all at once. Long-season crops include cucumber, eggplant, New Zealand spinach, peppers, pole beans, salsify, sweet potatoes, Swiss chard, and tomatoes.
6. Group short-season crops together for more convenient rotation and succession planting. They deplete the soil of nutrients more rapidly than do long-season crops. Such crops include radishes, lettuce, beets, carrots, bushbeans, and peas.
7. To save space, plant quick-growing vegetables between slow-growing vegetables, for example, radishes between rows of corn. The radishes are harvested long before the corn shades them and needs the space for its roots.
8. In a small garden, growing vine crops up a trellis or fence saves valuable ground space.
9. Most of a vegetable crop matures at about the same time. If you can't use fifty radishes all at once, plant some now, some in the next two weeks and then again two weeks later, to lengthen the harvest time. This is called *succession planting*, and it works well with many vegetables. Varieties of lettuce that mature at different times can be planted at the same time for a continuous harvest.
10. Timing is important when starting seeds indoors. If started too early, seedlings will be overgrown and won't easily adjust to outdoor conditions when transplanted. If started too late, the harvest will be delayed.

Opposite left: Cucuzzi, a fast-growing and rather exotic Chinese vegetable.
Opposite right: Grow different varieties of tomatoes to add to your garden pleasures. Pictured here, clockwise from the purple ruffled basil: 'Burpee's BIG BOY® Hybrid', 'Sweet 100 Hybrid' (cherry tomatoes), 'Yellow Pear', 'Lemon Boy VFN Hybrid', and 'Roma VF' (plum tomatoes).

DESIGNING A VEGETABLE GARDEN

STYLES OF VEGETABLE GARDENING

Vegetable gardens typically have been ostracized, stuck behind the garage or "out back," unseen by all but the gardener. But take another look. There is nothing ugly about a vegetable garden. In fact, there is great beauty. Take pride in your efforts. Step back occasionally and look at the big picture. Not since the days of the victory garden, when vegetables were not as readily available at the market, has the vegetable garden been much praised. Put a chair or bench and even a table by your garden. Take your morning coffee, your lunch, a drink to the garden, then sit and look around you. Contemplation will teach you to see more and make you a better gardener. It is a wonderful thing to be surrounded by plants and to celebrate the miracle of life. A traditional vegetable garden, with its straight rows planted in block formation, a tapestry of green punctuated by brightly colored vegetables, is not to be taken for granted or easily dismissed. It is no small accomplishment.

A traditional vegetable garden is laid out in rows which are spaced far enough apart to allow one person to walk between them in order to weed, water, and harvest the produce. This is a simple, practical, no-nonsense design.

For the new gardener, this is the easiest plan to execute the first year. Burpee's "Best Vegetable Garden" is an ideal plan with which to start. Plant it as shown here, or eliminate sections or substitute your favorite vegetables for those suggested. Just make sure to allow proper spacing between plants.

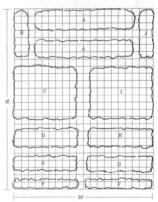

A. *Tomatoes*
B. *Pepper (Sweet), Crispy Hybrid*
C. *Zucchini, Burpee Hybrid*
D. *Cauliflower, Early White Hybrid*
E. *Carrot, Toudo Hybrid*
F. *Marigold, Fireworks Hybrid, Mixed Colors*
G. *Bush Beans, Tenderpod*
H. *Broccoli, Green Goliath*
I. *Cucumber, Bush*
J. *Eggplant, Burpee Hybrid*

Burpee's Best Vegetable Garden

A traditional vegetable garden growing at Williamsburg, Virginia.

THE ORNAMENTAL VEGETABLE GARDEN

Top: Peppers and Swiss chard are decorative growing alongside the annual flowers celosia and marigolds. Above: A formal vegetable garden is both beautiful and practical.

Vegetables and flowers can be combined in a garden that is both functional and ornamental. Vegetables are downright beautiful. Combine vegetables with flowers and create a garden of diverse greens, textures, and shapes that will please even the most discerning eye.

Vegetables and flowers are good companions, grown together for centuries for function and beauty. For example, early Americans knew marigolds repel harmful pests. Companion planting in vegetable gardening means encouraging a symbiotic—mutually beneficial—relationship between one plant and another. One plant may repel insects that commonly plague another.

Companion planting can be thought of in terms of pairings for beauty, too. Parsley, ruffled or plain, adds a wonderful, dark-green, textured border to a flower garden. As an edge to an early spring flower border, lettuce and cabbage are both attractive (but they will need to be replaced later when hot summer weather arrives). Thomas Jefferson grew tomatoes as a curiosity, an ornamental. He didn't eat them. Tomato plants add color and interest, and are a surprise when attractively surrounded by flowers.

Mother Nature didn't segregate vegetables and flowers in her garden. Why should we? Vegetables needn't be grown in seclusion by themselves, relegated to a plot behind the garage. More and more gardeners plant their vegetables near the house where they can be seen, enjoyed, and easily harvested.

With their sweet-pealike flowers and long, green pods, scarlet runner beans or any variety of peas growing on a fence or trellis behind a flower garden are both delicious and decorative.

The tall, ferny foliage of carrot tops or dill, planted so as to surround flowers with quite solid shapes (dahlias, lilies and daisies, for example), is very attractive; it frames and highlights the flowers. The tall, blue-green, spiky leaves of leeks, the red-tinged, wide leaves of beets, and the flaming red stems and leaves of Swiss chard can light up an ornamental garden with rich color and texture. Many root vegetables—carrots, radishes, and beets, among others—have interesting foliage. With their small, bulbous roots, they can be planted among your flowers without inconveniencing them in the least. As you harvest your vegetables, you make more room for the flowers to grow and expand over the summer. Try a mix of vegetables and flowers—even perennials—in a border. Combine different textures and colors of foliage that complement and enhance each other for a garden as beautiful as it is functional.

RAISED BEDS

Three years ago I introduced raised beds in my vegetable garden, and there are more benefits than I realized at the time.

The soil warms faster, I plant earlier, have better drainage, fewer weeds, and a more abundant harvest with more perfectly

shaped root crops. If I'd only known, I would have done it sooner.

A raised bed is simply a plot

raised above round level. You can mound soil eight to ten inches high in rows 1 to 1½ feet wide, level the top, and plant, or build it 1 to 1½ feet higher and wider, using a retaining wall around the perimeter. Some popular materials used to build the retaining walls are railroad ties and logs. The bed can be from 1 foot to 3 feet high, depending on whether you want to sit, kneel, or stand when working. A 3-foot-high raised bed allows handicapped people confined to wheelchairs easy access to work in their garden and can bring them many hours of pleasure and a feeling of accomplishment.

When building a retaining wall, keep in mind that the bin (growing area) should be no wider than twice the distance you can reach. That way, you can work the bed from either side without having to stand on and compress the soil. A raised-bed garden can consist of a single bed, a series of beds or a mix of different, geometrically shaped beds, arranged to fit neatly into your growing area. Triangles, squares, and even circles can be used very effectively. And, designed with various levels, and planted with cascading plants to spill over the edges and down the sides, a raised bed can be an dramatic addition to a terrace or yard, adding dimension, interest, and beauty—as well as ease of access—to your vegetable gardening.

CONTAINER GARDENING

One of the fastest growing hobbies for the gardener is container gardening. If you're an apartment- or city-dweller with a small yard, terrace, or balcony, you can have a wonderful vegetable garden. Just grow your tomatoes, peppers, cucumbers or eggplant in large pots or tubs. As long as the plants receive 6 to 8 hours of sun daily, they will do well, perhaps even better than if they had been planted in a garden, because they'll have the advantage of perfect soil. The dividends of container gardening include better protection from cold weather and frost, and a source of early maturing vegetables at a time when prices are still quite high at the market.

Sometimes, after planting your vegetables in the garden, you find you need just a bit more room for the leftovers. Like a child at supper, your eyes were bigger than your stomach, and you discover you can't fit one more tomato plant or that extra celery plant into the garden. The solution is to grow the extra vegetables in a container. Set them on the patio, the front steps, the front porch to greet your visitors or even beside the garden. Vegetables that need support or trellises can be grown in containers, too; anchor the planting stakes in the pot or place the pot next to a wall with a trellis, netting, or lattice attached. Peas and beans are lovely, and good candidates for growing against a house or garage. Of course, there's no reason why they have to grow *up*. They look splendid growing down out of a large container and trailing onto a terrace or porch. Herbs, of course, are wonder-

ful candidates for containers. If growing in containers is new to you, start simply. Don't take on so many containers that the pleasure becomes work. You can expand your efforts later when container gardening becomes a labor of love, as it surely will.

Consider, for the first year, growing 'Pixie Hybrid II', Burpee's prolific, small tomato that is quick to mature. Plant some basil around the tomato seedling, and at harvest time you can pick and use them together for everything from tomato sauce to salad. The next year, if you are feeling more ambitious, grow an entire salad garden, planting for spring, summer, and fall production. But walk before you run. We want you to enjoy all of your gardening.

Raised beds, like these above, allow for better drainage and easier weeding. Designed with curved edges, they can be decorative and especially attractive.

Pixie Hybrid II Tomatoes

Off-season vegetables are always a treat and a conversation stimulator, and one of the best is Burpee's 'Pixie Hybrid II'. This tomato is blissfully happy indoors, in pots and window boxes. It is a fast-growing variety and tops out at an average height of 18 inches.

Grown outdoors in the summer, 'Pixie Hybrid II' ripens in just over 50 days from the time seedlings are planted; indoor growth takes somewhat longer. Careful planning, per the chart below, can keep you in tasty, bright-scarlet tomatoes all year long. The 'Pixie Hybrid II' fruit is just under 2 inches across and is meatier than most small-fruited tomatoes.

Sow the seeds following the directions for planting indoors, cover lightly, and keep evenly moist at a temperature of 70 to 80 degrees Fahrenheit. Thin to one sturdy plant in each 8 × 8-inch or larger container by snipping off the extra plants once a second pair of leaves appears. (When thinning, do not pull up plants as this may upset the growth of the remaining seedling by disturbing the roots.)

This a good time to add sturdy stakes to provide support for the heavy fruit set. Plant the stake alongside the seedling stem far away enough to avoid contact with the roots. Tie up the branches with soft twine or strips of cloth as needed. Three stakes at the edge of the pot allow the growing plant more freedom to move; wrap loosely with string here too.

If you have room and good exposure, keep seedlings in full sun. Otherwise, light can be provided with fluorescent "grow" lights set 4 to 6 inches above the seedlings for 12 to 14 hours per day.

Setting the Fruit

As the flowers start to open, tap each cluster with your finger or a pencil. This will assure better pollination and fruit set. Tap the flowers in the midmorning when the pollen is less gummy. 'Pixie Hybrid II' plants are determinate—they mature at the same time—and for best production should not be pruned. Garden-grown Pixies will be larger than plants grown indoors. Pixies are good for eating out of hand and are excellent for tomato sauce.

PLANT SEEDS	START TO PICK FRUITS
Mid-July	October–November
October	February
Early January	April
March	July

A wide range of vegetables can be raised in containers. Pictured here: tomatoes in a hanging basket, beans, parsley, Swiss chard, leeks, and purple basil.

Container gardening doesn't have to stop when Jack Frost chases you indoors. Larger containers can be placed on wheels, and you can move them indoors. You can start new containers indoors, too, and grow some vegetables all winter in a sunny window or under lights.

Designing a Container Garden

Containers are wonderful places to explore garden design and plant combinations. No matter what size your container, it will be more attractive if something is spilling over the edges. The smaller containers are attractive with one plant variety, but large containers need to be planned. In a half whiskey barrel plant something bushy and upright in the center (like three 'Pixie Hybrid II' seedlings) and surround it with such cascading plants as nasturtiums. The contrast of growing habits will make your container look full, abundant, and more interesting. (In addition you'll have a more interesting salad if you include the flowers and pungent leaves of the nasturtium along with the tomatoes.) When combining plants, consider adding flowers for color and fragrance.

Our advice: mix and match. Grow radishes around a tomato plant or better yet, some lettuce. Or grow the radishes, which mature in about four weeks, harvest them, and then plant lettuce and basil. That way you can have three delightful salad ingredients mature at about the same time. A little planning, a little attention, and a large, fresh reward for your dinner table.

VEGETABLES RECOMMENDED FOR OUTDOOR CONTAINERS

VEGETABLE	VARIETY	MINIMUM CONTAINER SIZE—WIDTH AND DEPTH IN INCHES (1 plant per container unless noted)
Bean, Bush snap	'Burpee's Greensleeves'ⓥ	6 × 6 (2 each), 12 × 12 (4 each)
Bean, Pole snap	'Kentucky Wonder'	12 × 12 (2-4 plants on poles or trellis)
Bean, Pole lima	'King of the Garden'	12 × 12 (2-4 plants on poles or trellis)
Swiss Chard*	'Burpee's Fordhook® Giant'	6 × 6
	'Burpee's Rhubarb'	6 × 6
Cress	'Burpee's Curlycress'™	6 × 6 (broadcast seed)
Cucumber	'Burpee Hybrid'	12 × 12 (3 plants on trellis)
	'Burpless Hybrid'	12 × 12 (3 plants on trellis)
Eggplant	'Burpee's Black Beauty'	12 × 12
	'Burpee Hybrid'	12 × 12
Herbs	Chives*	6 × 6
	Oregano*	6 × 6
	Sweet Basil	6 × 6
	Sweet Marjoram	6 × 6
Lettuce*	'Burpee Bibb'	6 × 6
	'Green Ice'ᵛᴾ†	6 × 6
	'Oak Leaf'†	6 × 6
Parsley*†	'Extra Curled Dwarf'	6 × 6
Spinach*†	'Malabar'	8 × 8 (2 to 3 plants trailing or on trellis)
Strawberry†	'Baron Solemacher'	6 × 6
Summer Squash	'Burpee Golden Zucchini'ⓥ	12 × 12
	'Burpee Hybrid Zucchini'	12 × 12
Sweet Pepper	'California Wonder'	12 × 12
	'Sweet Banana'	12 × 12
Tomato	'Burpee's Pixie Hybrid II'†	8 × 8 (staked)
	'Burpee's Big Girl® Hybrid VF'	12 × 12 (on support)
	'Burpee's VF Hybrid'	12 × 12 (on support)
	'Basket Pak'†	12 × 12 (on support)
	'Red Cherry'†	12 × 12 (on support)
	'Yellow Plum'†	12 × 12 (on support)

*These varieties stand light frost;
all others cannot tolerate frost.
†Good for hanging baskets.
ⓥUnauthorized propagation prohibited—U.S. Variety.
   Protection applied for—U.S. Protected Variety.
   NOTE: Most need at least 6 hours of sunshine per day. The following may do well with less sunlight: Swiss Chard, 'Burpee's Curlycress', Lettuce, Parsley, and Spinach.

Care of Container Gardens

Take a moment to consider the advantages: Garden problems become small or almost nonexistent in a container. Since you'll use sterile soil, soil-borne diseases and insects, weeds, and bugs will not be present. A container garden requires less time, less physical energy, and less overall maintenance.

Container gardening does require a little daily or weekly attention, depending on how ambitious your project is. The seeds must be planted (or the nursery plants transplanted), then regularly watered, though lightly. As they begin to produce their fruits, fertilize with a weak water-soluble fertilizer when you water them. Eventually, they will be highly productive. Here is how to start.

Planting the Container Garden

First, choose a clean container. This may be anything that will hold soil and water, and in

A raised birdhouse serves as a focal point in a combination flower and vegetable garden.

which you can make a few drainage holes if there aren't any already, for drainage is essential to successful container gardening. A half-barrel, a small or large pot of clay or plastic or metal, a pail, a bushel basket, a wastebasket, a hanging basket, an old cake pan . . . you take it from there and use your imagination. Keep a close eye on smaller containers in sunny locations, as they will need more frequent watering.

If you use a bushel basket, or any basket, line it with sturdy plastic (a garbage bag is fine) slit with holes for drainage. This will help prevent over-watering, the most common cause of distress—and death—in container-grown plants. If you

choose a clay pot, be aware it will take more frequent watering because clay allows water to evaporate through the sides of the pot as well as out the top. Fill with potting soil.

Fit the plant (or plants) to the pot. Peppers, cucumbers, cantaloupe, tomatoes, squash, and watermelon grow roots to a depth of 12 or more inches; the roots of lettuce, greens, and radishes grow to 8 inches; spinach, rhubarb, onion, bean, pea, beet, and Swiss chard roots are somewhere in between, with roots reaching about 8 to 12 inches.

This means that you can't plant a tomato seedling, or tomato seeds, in an 8-inch-deep pot. Nor should you waste a

12-inch-deep pot on a 4- to 6-inch radish root. But for every typical, backyard vegetable, there is a suitable pot to place on your porch, patio, balcony, or in that sunny window with the southern exposure.

In hot, dry, or windy weather, you may need to water once or even twice a day to prevent drying out. Hybrids are often a good choice for container growing, since they may offer dwarf varieties or plants with dwarf habits. Growing plants such as tomatoes, cucumbers, or pole beans in containers requires a strong pole or trellis for support, so plan ahead. Essentially, the care of container plants is similar to that of garden plants.

CHILDREN'S GARDENING

Katie Bales and her dog, Buffy, enjoy lazy summer afternoons playing in a teepee covered with vines of scarlet runner beans, peas, and morning glories.

Give a child the gift of working with Mother Nature. It will be the start of a love that will last a lifetime. The miracle of seeds that grow into huge pumpkins, tall sunflowers or tiny carrots and Jack Be Little pumpkins small enough to fit in the hand, will tickle and excite children. A garden is a wonderful thing to share with children—yours, your neighbors', or those of friends.

There are many fun garden activities you can share pleasantly with a child. The patience and attention span of children are short, and with young children it is best to make gardening light-hearted, rather than a drudgery. Let them come and go in the garden as they please, and play around in the dirt or mud (a favorite activity

of children through the ages).

Activities with quick or surprising results really capture a child's attention. Red radishes germinate quickly and can be eaten in about four weeks. Plant a variety of radishes—red, white, long, short, and fat—and you will create a learning experience to delight children with a new shape and color every time they pull a radish from the ground. (See whether they can match the radish to its name—'Easter Egg', 'French Breakfast', 'White Icicle', 'Cherry Bomb', and so on.)

Sunflowers also germinate quickly to stand at attention, towering over kids, in about eight weeks. As the plants grow ever taller, the kids will have to crick their heads back to see the sunflower's face. There are

many ways to use sunflower seeds, all of them fun and educational. Seeds can be left for the birds, of course, or harvested, dried, roasted, and eaten.

Starting seeds indoors is a fun activity for a rainy day near the end of winter. Every step is an education: puffing the peat pellet with water, planting the seed, watering and misting, transplanting, and harvesting. But the most fun for children is when they first see the seedlings pop out of the soil.

Encourage children to touch plants (gently, of course), to smell the flowers and the fruit, and to pick and eat right from the vine. Scarlet runner beans are especially enchanting. Children love to watch the red flowers change and grow into beans, and are thrilled on opening the green pod to find bright, scarlet-red beans inside.

Scarecrows really don't frighten away birds very well, but they give a garden personality and visitors a chuckle. Children enjoy dressing them, naming them, and even talking to them.

The wildlife in a garden is another source of interest to children, from the "ugh" reserved for slugs to the "oohs" for the butterflies. Hopping after toads (if you're lucky enough to have them—they help control your insect population), chasing ladybugs, and even picking slow-moving caterpillars and Japanese beetles off leaves and into a glass bottle, are learning activities for children and are to be encouraged. Order friendly, beneficial insects and earthworms through the mail and let your children release them in the garden to help control harmful insects.

The activities for children are countless and as you play with them in the garden they will find new ones on their own. Add them to this list and perhaps share them with us. Here's a start:

1. Grow different varieties of the same vegetables, for example, red, pink, and yellow tomatoes; giant and tiny pumpkins; speckled, yellow, and pink corn (all good for popping).
2. Carve a child's name in the outer skin of a pumpkin when it is young and then watch as the name grows in size with the pumpkin.
3. Grow the crazy and grotesque gourds; children will be intrigued. They can paint faces on them.
4. Try some of the unusually colored vegetables. They will make an interesting treat for the whole family; golden beets, rainbow corn, purple cabbage. 'Royal Burgundy' beans have purple pods that turn green when cooked (it must be magic).
5. Let one zucchini grow to baseball-bat size, then use it for soup.
6. Help your child grow a cucumber inside a narrow-necked glass bottle and surprise friends who won't know how you did it. This is the same effect as model ships in bottles. A baby cucumber can easily be slipped into the bottle; once inside, it can grow to full size. The bottle

will act as a greenhouse, holding and intensifying the heat of the sun to such a degree that it will rot the cucumber if the bottle isn't shaded (use cucumber leaves or old newspapers). Cut the cucumber from the vine when it has almost filled the bottle. If you like, you can preserve it by pickling it right in the bottle.
7. Children love silly names and they are easy to remember. Here is a list of varieties with funny names. Children can make up a story about how the vegetable or flower got its name; they'll probably be right.

'Pickalot Hybrid' cucumber
'French Breakfast' radish
'Green Goliath' broccoli
'Little Finger' carrot
'Sweet Dream Hybrid' melon
'Clown Mix' torenia
'Madness' petunia
'Fluffy Ruffles' aster
Snapdragons
Polka-dot plant
'Naughty Marietta' marigold
'Sweet Banana' peppers
'Turk's Turban' gourd
'Red Sails' loose-leaf lettuce
'Burpless' cucumber

Top: Mammoth sunflowers grow up to 12 feet very quickly, in less than three months. Above: Making a scarecrow of their own is a fun project for children.

SELECTING SEEDS

Hybrid and Open-pollinated Seeds

At Burpee we are frequently asked why some seeds are more expensive than others. The answer is that hybrid seeds are more expensive to produce than open-pollinated varieties. Hybrid varieties are particularly easy to grow and harvest, and

there are many wonderful varieties available at good prices.

Hybrid seeds are produced by crossing two different parents, and will grow only one generation of plants. The offspring from a hybrid revert to resemble the parentage, so saving seed from hybrids is not recommended. All hybrids are so noted on seed packs, and

"hybrid" is part of the seed name. Each year the Burpee growers must cross-pollinate the same parents and harvest new seed to achieve the same superior results. The process is not complicated but, for some varieties, it is labor-intense.

In the case of some hybrids, cucumbers and squash, for example, male and female plants

The Story of a Tomato Hybrid

A tomato flower has both female and male parts. A breeder will designate some tomatoes to be the female plant. These "females" are staked for easy identification when pollinating and harvesting. Field workers then remove the anthers—the male organ—from these tomato flowers to prevent the tomato from self-pollinating.

Flowers are then collected from other, "male" plants of the same variety and these flowers are dried on screens set out in the sun. When the pollen is dry, it is shaken from the flowers and stored under refrigeration to keep it fresh until ready to use.

Pollination of tomatoes is done by hand. When the female flower turns yellow and blooms, seedsmen have a day or at the most two to pollinate that flower. Workers dip the stigma—the female organ—into a glass pollinating tube (designed by Burpee). The stigma is covered with pollen, then marked by removing three sepals surrounding the flower. This is done so that, when they return to harvest the tomatoes, they can identify and pick only those hand-pollinated. As many as twenty-two workers per acre spend five to six weeks pollinating one tomato hybrid.

The story doesn't end there. After harvest, the tomatoes are crushed and fermented, the seeds separated from the pulp, washed, dried, and bagged. Only then are the seeds ready to package for the home gardener.

are planted in adjacent rows and the bees pollinate and cross-pollinate them. For others like tomatoes and cantaloupe, pollination must be done carefully by hand.

Why develop hybrids? What the breeders are looking for in a new, hybrid vegetable variety and what the gardener wants in a vegetable are the same.

Good flavor is first and foremost. Vegetables that appear in supermarkets, tomatoes in particular, are grown from seeds bred to meet the commercial growers' criteria. The commercial grower wants his vegetables to ripen together so he can harvest the entire field more economically at one time. He prefers good keeping quality, which may result in tough skins. Take the case of tomatoes. The commercial grower wants them to ripen slowly after being picked green, so they last when on the road to the supermarket, instead of being sun-ripened on the vine. All of this accounts for the difference in taste between home-grown and commercially grown varieties.

There are advantages beyond better flavor which the home gardener enjoys. Disease resistance is one of them. Look for the letters V, F, or N, appearing after variety names, in catalogs and on seed packs. They tell the home gardener that these varieties are resistant to verticillium wilt, fusarium wilt and nematodes. Concern for the environment has encouraged breeding for disease resistance, allowing us good results without using harmful chemicals.

Lots of new varieties are heavy yielders that produce more than the older varieties, so the home gardener can enjoy more produce from less space. Space-saving plants, the dwarf varieties, mean that a heavily producing plant can fit in a container garden, and you can grow more plants in a small garden, for a larger harvest from less space.

MINIATURE OR BABY VEGETABLES

The popularity of miniature vegetables is on the increase. In big city areas, commercial growers supply these little morsels to fresh produce markets where they command a very high price to compensate the grower for the smaller yield in pounds per acre.

Baby vegetables tend to be milder and more tender than their fully grown sisters. As a home gardener, you can pick and serve some of the vegetables you grow as baby vegetables and allow others in the same crop to mature to full size.

The tiny ears of corn used in Chinese cuisine can be harvested from any sweet corn variety. When tassels—the male portion of the flower—appear on the top of your corn plants, you know that the silks—the female part—are about to appear. Watch closely and you'll see that only a few days after tassels come the silks. Just pick the tiny ears of corn within two or three days of silking. Pick okra young, and pick any summer squash within 24 hours of flowering. Zucchini should be no more than 4 inches long. Even delicious "new" potatoes fit into this second category.

When selecting vegetables to harvest as "babies," buy only recommended varieties. Some vegetables, when picked early, lack the vitamins, sweetness, and flavor that develop only as the vegetables mature. Fortunately there are some baby vegetables which we heartily recommend, bred for their small size and, when mature, provide the nutrition and flavor their bigger cousins do.

You can grow many "true" baby vegetables in your garden. The following is a list of baby vegetables plus those vegetables which can be picked while immature. All are mild, tender, and full of vitamins, sweetness, and flavor.

Beets
  'Little Ball'
  'Burpee Golden'
Carrots
  'Short and Sweet'
  'Little Finger'
Cucumber
  'Pickling Cucumbers'
Eggplant
  'Millionaire'
Kohlrabi
  'Grand Duke'
Lettuce
  'Romaine, Little Gem'
  'Burpee Bibb'
Onion
  'Crystal Wax Pickling PPR'
Okra
  'Clemson Spineless'
  'Annie Oakley Hybrid'
Pea
  'Snowbird'

Pumpkin
  'Jack Be Little'
Radish
  'Cherry Belle'
  'Burpee White'
Summer Squash
  'Burpee Hybrid Zucchini'
  'Richgreen Hybrid Zucchini'
  'Burpee Golden Zucchini'
  'Pic-N-Pic Hybrid'
  'Sunburst Hybrid'
Tomato
  'Gardener's Delight'
  'Pixie Hybrid II'
  'Yellow Pear'
  'Sundrop'
  'Sweet 100'
Turnip
  'Tokyo Cross'
  'Purple-top'
  'White Globe'

THE VEGETABLE PLANTING AND GROWING GUIDE

SEEDS

The promise of seeds is the miracle of life in multicolored, multisized, and multishaped packages. Hold a seed in your hand and ponder for a moment: That tiny seed has the complete nutrients to sprout. It will grow to a thousand times its size, needing only moisture and fertilizer after waking from its dormant state. Some seeds, those of tomatoes for example, will last for 18 or 20 years if kept cool and dry in their dormant state; since the percent of viable seeds decreases over time, though, we recommend using fresh seed whenever possible. Other seeds, like lettuce and parsnip, last for a year, longer if given special care and sealed in foil packs. All seeds, though similar, have individual characteristics and needs; some are fussier and more demanding than others.

Today seeds are readily available and we take them for granted. When Europeans arrived on this continent hundreds of years ago with their few belongings, one of their most precious was seeds. Seeds were so valuable that they substituted for money. Seeds were bartered for tools, household goods, and animals. They were even a welcome wedding present. Every early American garden included a small patch where vegetables were allowed to go to seed. These were used for the next year's crop and exchanged with friends and neighbors, so each settler could increase the number of varieties he grew. Crops that matured the second year, carrots, beets, and potatoes, were carefully protected from mice, damp, and cold over the winter, then replanted in the spring to produce seed.

For many early Americans, the garden was their life. The more crops they grew, the better prepared they were for winter, and the better able they were to barter for the things they needed. Today, the hardest part of growing from seeds is choosing what to grow. The variety available is enormous and the quality improves with every year. Of course, the kinds of seeds you choose will determine where and how you plant them. You can start some seeds indoors to gain extra weeks on the growing season. Some seeds are best sown right into the garden, fast-germinating vegetables like leaf lettuce and mustard greens, for example. Other kinds of vegetables don't always do well when transplanted, so their seeds should be direct sown where they are to grow. Among these are beans and root crops like beets and carrots. Wait for the ground to begin to warm, then plant the seeds of these tender plants directly in the soil. Refer to our Plant Portraits section, page 41, or the back of your seed pack for the needs of individual seeds.

Vines, such as the melons here, look welcoming and lush spilling out across a walkway.

Seeds are astonishingly diverse in size and color. 1. Snap pea 'Snappy ☻' 2. Cucumber 'Burpeeana Hybrid II' 3. Corn 'Kandy Korn E.H.' 4. Onion 'Evergreen Long White Bunching.' 5. Pumpkin 'Big Max' 6. Squash 'Burpee Hybrid Zucchini' 7. Lettuce 'Parris Island Cos' 8. Watermelon 'Sweet Favorite Hybrid' 9. Tomato 'Super Beefsteak ☻ VFN' 10. Beet 'Detroit Dark Red' 11. Pepper 'Crispy Hybrid' 12. Pole lima bean 'Burpee's Best' 13. Snap bean 'Improved Evergreen' 14. Cabbage 'Earliana' 15. Snap bean 'Burpee's Tenderpod' 16. Corn 'Rainbow' 17. Bush fava bean 'Long Pod' 18. Carrot 'Toudo Hybrid' 19. Radish 'White Chinese' 20. Eggplant 'Early Beauty' 21. Cauliflower 'Early White Hybrid' 22. Cantaloupe 'Hale's Best Jumbo'.

STARTING SEEDS INDOORS

By sowing Bibb lettuce or cucumbers indoors (even though they can be direct sown in the garden), you can enjoy your crop weeks earlier and weeks longer, stretching the season.

Some plants take a long time to mature. In most climates, tomatoes, peppers, and eggplants direct sown outdoors after the weather has warmed enough may not have time to produce ripened fruit before the fall frost. If you are a northern gardener, indoor sowing or purchase of bedding plants for some varieties is a necessity due to a short

growing season. In this case, it's also wise to choose quick-bearing varieties of vegetables; your seed catalog will tell you which to choose, the dates for planting, and the time to maturity for your zone. On the other hand, cool-weather crops, especially the cabbage family in some parts of the country, need an indoor start in early spring to give them enough time to mature before the onset of hot summer weather. Often such adverse weather conditions as extremely wet, cold, dry, or hot weather may hinder outdoor

seeding. Starting seeds indoors will beat the adverse weather and produce plants that are ready to transplant when the weather improves.

Indoor sowing makes more effective use of limited space in the small garden. It allows double cropping in the same space, the second crop following the harvest of the first, thereby increasing your yield of vegetables for the table.

Some small seeds are difficult to handle outdoors. Tiny seeds can be started indoors more easily than out where wind, birds, and heavy rain can be a hindrance. They're much easier to handle indoors, out of the wind.

Expensive seeds can be grown more effectively when started indoors where they will be protected from heavy rains and temperature fluctuations. Small hybrid seeds, for example, produce more plants per packet when sown indoors under controlled conditions.

Double cropping: When you're waiting for room in your garden for a second crop, have the seedlings ready to go into the ground as soon as the first crop is harvested. Time the second crop by growing it indoors to the seedling stage. This is called "double cropping," and it ensures that no growing time is lost. For example, indoor-started cabbage seedlings can be transplanted for a fall crop as soon as bean crops are harvested in the summer, and the amount of time they will need to grow in the garden will be shortened.

Don't forget the advantages of early greenhouse sowing of vegetables destined for the outdoor garden! Some varieties, especially in northern areas, need to be started indoors in order to mature when the weather is most favorable. Follow the cultural directions on Burpee seed packets, and time your plantings according to the climate in your area. If necessary, provide warm soil conditions for best germination.

Remember that it's necessary to harden off plants before setting them outside in their permanent garden location. To harden off plants, gradually accustom them to outdoor condi-

tions by moving the young plants to a protected spot outside about one week before transplanting time. Shelter them in the greenhouse or covered cold frame at night if temperatures drop near freezing. Don't allow young plants to dry out; be especially watchful on windy or very sunny days when gardens dry out faster.

The proper time to sow seeds indoors depends on your climate and the growing time for your plants, and is figured from the dates of the last spring frost for your area. Some plants are hardier than others and can be transferred to the garden earlier in spring—as soon as the ground can be prepared. These plants can stand a light frost. Some seeds take a long time to sprout, and some plants take a longer time to grow to transplant size. All of these factors determine when to sow seeds indoors. Fortunately, the information you need to sow on a timely basis is on the seed packet and in the charts in this chapter. Enter the information in your notebook. Keep the average date of the last frost for your local area and then plan from the first date backward. In the garden, identify your seeds with a marker with the date planted and the time needed for growth to transplant size.

When starting seeds indoors, you can plant with a complete starter kit (you might try Burpee's Seed N' Start™), or with peat pellets that contain a special planting mix with nutrients for the young seedlings. You can use and reuse plastic or wooden trays, 2 to 4 inches deep, which permit planting many seeds in a row, three or four rows wide.

You can even recycle plastic or cardboard milk cartons, egg cartons, metal cans, disposable drinking cups, or other objects as seed-starting containers. Whatever is handy will work, but if you improvise or reuse containers, you must clean them well to eliminate soil-borne disease, and you must poke holes in the bottom to provide good drainage. (To clean, use one part laundry bleach to nine parts water and soak for 5 minutes.)

Get seeds off to a successful start with:

. . . sufficient water, good air circulation, light, and proper temperature. Some seeds need cooler sprouting temperatures than others (check your notes or refer to the seed packet or the "Plant Portraits," page 41).

. . . adequate light immediately after sprouts appear. Seedlings grow weak and leggy if light is inadequate.

. . . good planting medium. For starting your seeds indoors, keep in mind that a good planting medium, one that is porous for good drainage, well-aerated, and free of weed seeds and harmful organisms, is indispensable. It's available from your garden catalog, garden center, or nursery. Soil-less growing media can be vermiculite, perlite, or a combination with peat moss for a mix that is light with good aeration and water retention (but contains no plant food). Mixtures of perlite, vermiculite (for aeration and water retention), and sphagnum peat moss (also for water retention) plus a combination of slow-release and fast-release fertilizers to get the seedlings off to a good start are available. Burpee's Tomato Formula for tomatoes, peppers, and eggplant, and Burpee's Planting Formula for all other seeds, are two of these. A soil-less mix is also light in weight, nice when plants in containers have to be moved around.

Fill the cleaned pots, flats, or containers with moistened planting mix. Moistening the planting mix is most easily done right in the bag by adding water at the rate of 1 quart of water to 6 quarts of formula; retie the bag and shake vigorously to distribute water evenly, then let it drain. If using large flats or trays, sow seed sparingly in shallow furrows 2 to 3 inches apart or according to the instructions on the seed packet, and cover lightly with planting medium. Allow plenty of space between seeds so they won't become too crowded before they are thinned or transplanted. Crowding will produce weak, spindly seedlings and encourages the spread of disease. Give seeds the room they need as they grow their roots and whatever the seed size, be sure to follow the planting directions on the seed packet.

In addition to keeping an informal record in your garden notebook, mark and label each variety of planted seeds with a plant stake, as it's difficult to tell one plant type from another when the seedlings first emerge.

Once your seeds are planted in the moist planting mix, you need only wet the seed and soil surface with a fine spray of water. Then seal the entire container inside a clear plastic bag, which will produce a greenhouse effect and prevent evaporation as it holds in warmth. If the planting mix begins to dry out, mist carefully, but do not disturb the seeds. Too much moisture at the soil level can cause damping off, where potential seedlings die at the soil level. To avoid overheating, keep the covered container out of direct sunlight.

As soon as the first seeds have sprouted, remove the plastic cover. Temperature is important in the early stages of seed growing. Seeds germinate at different temperatures, but most do well between 70 and 75 degrees Fahrenheit. Consider using one of the electric, indoor bottom-heating trays especially designed to maintain the appropriate temperature for starting seeds. Models with adjustable and fixed temperature controls are readily available at garden centers and from garden catalogs. If you use heat, your plants will emerge more quickly, and once they do, you must provide good light. Keep the flats or containers in a warm, draft-free place. If you do not have enough room for the seedlings in a sunny window, use fluorescent lights.

In large flats, group your plants so that slow-germinating types share one flat and the fast-germinating types share another. Don't mix fast- and slow-germinating seeds in one container, because you want them to be ready for transplanting at the same time.

When the planting mix surface begins to dry out, water your plants carefully with a mister. If more water is needed, stand the containers in a tray of water until the mix becomes saturated from the bottom up, then, remove the containers from the tray of water and allow to drain thoroughly. Never let the planting mix dry out completely.

Artificial Light

If you don't have a window with a southern exposure and strong enough sunlight to produce good seedlings, you can use a fluorescent light. Even with good southern exposure, if your plants are in the windowsill, a long spell of cloudy weather could interfere with good growth. Most of the time it's necessary to provide additional lighting so seedlings receive enough light for healthy plant growth. Although artificial light does not duplicate sunlight, there are lights that produce the right combination of waves to stimulate good growth in plants. Incandescent bulbs, while high in red light, are low in the blue and violet ranges. Incandescent bulbs can burn hot enough to destroy young seedlings if placed too close, and we don't recommend using them.

Ordinary fluorescent lights are best. They produce almost no heat and the seedlings can be set close to the lights so the plants receive strong, steady light. Results using fluorescent light are very good. The seedlings should be kept 4 to 6 inches beneath the lights for 12 to 18 hours per day. You can use a timer to turn them off at night and on again the next morning. Remember: Provide good air circulation and never let the planting mix dry out completely.

It is not true that seedlings need a period of darkness each day. At Burpee, some gardeners grow their seeds under lights twenty-four hours a day when they want faster growth. The low-intensity lights give the plants only as much light as they can absorb. The only danger with using lights 'round the clock is that the seedlings need to be watched more closely; they will need more water, and more frequently will have to be moved to maintain the right distance (4 to 6 inches) between the light and the top of the plants.

To avoid leggy, spindly seedlings:

- Sow thinly; if leaves overlap, thin right away.

- Provide full light as soon as seedlings emerge.

- Keep seedlings slightly dry; avoid wilting, but do not overwater.

- Keep temperatures on the cool side once seedlings appear; growth will be slower but plants sturdier.

- Allow for good air circulation (but avoid drafts).

Fertilizing Seedlings

Seedlings don't need a lot of fertilizer, particularly if a planting mix that contains compost or plant food is used. Over-fertilized seedlings put too much effort into growing lush foliage and won't produce good vegetables. If you sow your seeds in a soil-less medium (vermiculite or perlite), transplant the seedlings promptly to a rich planting mix or add a weak fertilizer when watering to provide nutrients. (Remember, some soil-less media also contain slow-release fertilizer. With these, you needn't fertilize until you transplant the seedlings into the garden.) After three or four weeks' growth, seedlings can be fed with a weak solution of balanced fertilizer, according to the manufacturer's directions.

TRANSPLANTING TO THE GARDEN

Start hardening off—accustoming the seedlings to the outdoors—about a week before transplanting them to the garden (after all danger of frost). Leave them outside in a cold frame, or place them out in a partially protected place for an extended time each day, starting with about eight hours the first day, and adding an hour per day of exposure. After a week or ten days, they will be ready to transplant. The lengthening time outdoors will toughen the cell structure and reduce transplant shock so your seedlings will better adjust to their new environment when planted outside.

Whether you grow your own seedlings or purchase started plants from a nursery, the transplanting method is the same.

First to be transplanted to the garden are the hardy vegetables, such as broccoli, onions, cabbage, and Chinese cabbage. They can be carefully transferred to their permanent garden location as soon as the ground can be worked in the spring and the danger of heavy frost is past. Tender varieties must wait until all danger of frost, light or heavy, is over and the ground begins to warm.

It is preferable to do all of your transplanting late in the afternoon on a cloudy and windless day. Don't allow the plant roots to dry out while waiting to be set into the garden.

Set the plants into the soil at a slightly deeper level than they were in the pots or tray. (For tomatoes, the soil level should come just under the first pair of leaves.) Firm the soil around the base of the plants, but be careful you don't injure the stems. If you use peat pellets or peat pots, gently break the bottom of the peat pot or remove the plastic mesh from the pellet so it is easier for the roots to penetrate into the garden soil; sink each peat pellet or pot deep enough to cover the top completely. Otherwise, the sun can dry them out, and the plant roots too.

If frosts or cold temperatures are predicted, cover the plants at night with newspapers, plastic tents, a plant blanket (also known as a garden blanket and floating row cover) or hotkaps for protection. (A hotkap is an individual hothouse of weather-resistant waxed paper, available at garden centers and from garden catalogs.) Remove coverings—except plant blankets—during the day so that heat does not build up and kill the seedlings. The plant blanket can stay on night and day. It allows good air circulation and light to permit the plants to grow unimpeded underneath it. When the temperature outside reaches 80 degrees Fahrenheit, take the blanket off and fold it up for use next year.

DIRECT SOWING IN THE GARDEN

Some vegetables have large or quick-germinating seed, and it is preferable to direct sow them. Peas, beans, corn, and radishes are examples. Some vegetables do not transplant easily, or they mature so quickly that they are best direct sown in the garden. The time to direct sow in the garden depends on two things: the individual kinds of vegetables chosen and the average date of the last frost of the area of the country in which you live.

As a rule, hardy types that can withstand some cool weather are planted in the fall in southern and West Coast areas. In regions with cold winters, frost-hardy vegetables are planted in spring when the heavy frost is over and the soil can be worked or, for a fall crop, in midsummer so they mature before the extremely cold weather arrives. Tender classes of vegetables should be planted when all danger of frost is over and the soil is warming. Examples of frost-hardy vegetables include spinach, peas, turnips, mustard, collards, and kale.

When seeds are direct sown into the garden, care must be taken to prevent the soil from drying out and forming a crust. Sometimes this crust is so hard it's impossible for tiny seedlings to emerge. During normal spring weather there is usually enough moisture in the soil to foster quick germination, but in summer, soil dries out fast. You can prevent the soil from crusting by covering it with vermiculite and keeping the seedbed evenly moist, or by sowing seeds in shallow-dug trenches filled with vermiculite, sand, or a light, porous soil mix friendly to young, tender plants and which will not crust.

If you are planting your vegetables in rows, you'll want them to be straight rows. Cut a length of string a foot longer than the row. Tie each end to a stick (or pencil). Poke one stick into the ground at the beginning of the row, and the other at the end. Make a trench (at the appropriate depth for your seed) in the soil, using the string as a guide.

When seedlings are large enough to handle (usually when they have two pairs of true leaves), thin to the distances recommended on the seed packets. Some leafy crops (lettuce and Chinese cabbage, for example) can be thinned progressively and the thinnings used in salads.

Seed Tapes

Burpee's seed tapes make gardening easier than ever. The seeds are attached at the proper spacing to 15-foot paper tapes. The tape disintegrates after planting.

Seed tapes:

♦ make it easy to handle seeds.

♦ allow uniform emergence of vigorous seedlings.

♦ give seedlings the space they need for early growth.

♦ reduce the time, work, and loss involved in thinning seedlings.

♦ allow enough room for healthy root systems to develop, minimizing transplanting risks.

♦ permit sowing in perfectly straight rows or in any other formation desired.

A garden blanket speeds germination and protects seeds from insects.

♦ may be cut at any point for multiple row planting or to be saved for a second sowing.

When referring to planting dates, the two most important are the last frost date in the spring and the first in the fall. Other significant dates are those of the last heavy frost, the last light frost, and when all danger of frost is past.

Frost is moisture that freezes on or within foliage. Local environmental conditions including cloud cover, altitude, air movement, and humidity determine when frost will occur. It is likely to develop anytime after sundown when temperatures drop below 40 degrees Fahrenheit. As the temperature nears 32 degrees Fahrenheit, moisture in the air condenses and forms white crystals on foliage; this is "light frost," which will damage only tender plants. A heavy or "killing" frost occurs when temperatures drop low enough to freeze the moisture within the foliage, which then wilts and dies.

Relatively hardy varieties such as cabbage, beets, and lettuce may be set out in the garden after the last heavy frost. They like cool weather and can stand a light frost. Tender varieties of vegetables, such as tomatoes, cucumbers, and beans, must wait until *all* danger of frost is past. Many crops can be grown in fall, if planted in summer early enough so they may be harvested before the first fall frost damages them. Crops such as kale, collards, and leeks can withstand heavy frost and can, in fact, be harvested during the winter if not frozen too firmly in the ground.

Cold Frame

If you plan to start a good many seeds prior to transplanting them into your garden, there is nothing more satisfactory and helpful, short of a greenhouse, than a cold frame. You can buy a finished cold frame, one ready to assemble from a kit or as a partial kit with the hardware and specifications for the lumber needed, or you can make your own cold frame from an old storm window and whatever used lumber you might have lying around in your garage or basement. Cold frames have a top-to-bottom slant to invite the southern sun into every corner of the box. Window orientation should be slanted toward the south.

A cold frame allows you to plant your seeds outside the house, eliminate clutter inside, and keep your seed germinating and your seedlings growing even through a frost or two. When the top is closed, the temperature inside is enough higher than outside to keep plants from freezing. It's a good idea to hang a thermometer inside to keep tabs on the temperature. If there is a dramatic drop anticipated (a freeze coming), throw a tarpaulin or old blanket over the entire cold frame to beat the freeze and save the plants. The addition of a little newspaper under the tarpaulin or blanket gives additional heat and protection. At the other extreme, when the sun gets hot it can roast the plants, so keep the top open during the day when the temperature outside the cold frame gets to 60 degrees Fahrenheit. Some manufactured cold frames come with automatic thermostats that open the cold frame on hot days and close it on cold days to control the temperature.

Hot Bed

A hot bed is a cold frame with a heating unit under the soil or around the sides of the box. These are usually automatically controlled. The addition of heat to the cold frame converts it to a miniature greenhouse and adds to its versatility. If you have a source of fresh horse manure, you can create a hot bed by burying 8 inches of manure under 6 inches of soil. The heat provided by the composting manure will heat the cold frame and keep frost out.

Gardener's Gold

The condition of the soil is the single most important factor in gardening. A healthy soil discourages disease, grows strong plants to survive insect attacks and encourages abundant crops. More problems or disappointments stem from poor soil preparation than from any other cause. If your soil is not properly prepared, you're finished before you've even begun. The better the soil, the better the harvest. All plants need air, water, and nutrients from the soil in order to grow. Every soil needs preparation every year. The preparation steps to take depend on the type of soil. There are three basic types: clay, loam, and sand.

Clay soil

Sandy soil

Loamy soil

CLAY: A potter's pleasure but a gardener's nightmare. The particles of clay soil hold water and force out air, forming a solid mass that is slow to dry out and when it does, becomes rock hard. When organic matter is worked into clay soil, the clay will effectively hold the nutrients that vegetables need to grow.

SAND: Ideal at the beach but trouble in the garden. Sand particles leave plenty of space for air but water and nutrients wash right out, making it hard for all but very drought-tolerant plants to survive.

LOAM: Gardener's gold. This is what we all strive for. Somewhere between clay and sand, containing organic material that gives it a fluffy, light texture. The best soil in any garden is the top few inches where decaying plant roots, leaves and other organic matter naturally decay. This is called the top soil. For a vegetable garden more than for any other kind of garden, you need a deep loam 8 or 12 inches deep. Loamy soils are physically easy to prepare, and weeding and watering are easier too.

This isn't difficult to achieve, but will be more time-consuming the first year than in years to come. Every year compost will have to be dug into the soil. As you continue to grow crops, they deplete the soil of nutrients which must be replenished. Compost adds nutrients, increases water retention, and is light enough to allow air to stay in the soil.

Steps for Preparing the Soil

Like all living things, plants need air, water, and sunshine—and two of these three reach the plants through the soil. The better the soil, the better the harvest.

Whether preparing a new garden or readying the soil of an established one, you start by spading or rototilling the soil to at least spade depth, 8 to 10 inches. This loosens and aerates the soil, providing a good home for your crops and assuring their development and healthy growth. Whenever possible, begin the preparation of your garden in the fall.

"Top dress" the garden with your choice of humus-building materials: compost, peat moss, manure. Rototill or spade the garden again to mix and improve the soil, and carry the nutrients down to the depth that the vegetable roots will reach.

Also, if you've dug away some of the lawn to enlarge your vegetable plot, be sure to remove all of the grass from the area. Grass grows so quickly as to crowd out seedlings. You can either bury it a foot deep in your garden to add nutrients to the soil as it decomposes or throw it on your compost pile.

Come spring, continue your efforts to improve your soil. Vegetable gardens need yearly replenishment of nutrients and humus; what you take out, you must give back. If you did not add fertilizer in the fall, now is the time to do so, but a word of warning . . . don't work the soil when it is wet; wait until the surface has begun to dry out

and the soil below the surface is only moist. Working with soil when it's too wet can ruin its structure by compacting the particles, and this kind of damage can take a long time to correct. If you live in an area of the country known for its mud season, you should prepare soil in the fall. You'll add weeks of growing to your season because you won't have to wait for the soil to dry out before it can be planted. Raised beds are also a good solution to mud problems, providing better drainage and allowing the soil to warm more quickly.

TESTING THE SOIL: For the tastiest vegetables possible at harvest time, test the condition of the soil. That is the best way to find out what it needs to bring it to its most fertile state for the seeds or seedlings it will nourish and grow.

A soil test is easy. You can buy a simple, inexpensive soil kit or, if you prefer, arrange a complete soil test from an independent laboratory, your local county extension service, or agricultural college. A complete soil test will evaluate the nutrients in the soil and the pH. You can buy a pH meter yourself, to test for acidity or alkalinity in the soil. Put the prongs into the soil and you get an instant reading. The reading will tell you if your soil is acid (sour) or alkaline (sweet). This condition is rated on a scale of 1 to 14. As a general rule, most soils east of the Mississippi River are slightly acid, while most soils west of the Mississippi are alkaline.

Take readings at different

locations in the garden, since soil condition varies even from one spot to the next in your own backyard. Collect topsoil samples from different spots and mix the samples together. You'll need about 8 ounces of soil to make your tests. (If you send the samples to your County Extension Agent, they'll want to know what plants you'll be growing in that soil.) Your test results will show a pH reading and tell you how much lime or sulfur to add per 100 square feet to bring the condition to ideal. Generally, soils do not vary too far from neutral and need only minor adjustments in pH. For growing vegetables, you will want a pH reading of around 6.5 or slightly sour (between 6 and 7 is fine). Because both lime and sulfur work slowly, it's best to incorporate one or the other into the topsoil in the fall; over the winter months, they will adjust the condition of the soil.

FEEDING THE SOIL: Gardeners often refer to the "tilth" of their soil, by which they mean the physical condition that enables it to support good plant growth. Good soil should be friable (free from caking) and have a high content of organic matter for good plant nutrition and root aeration. The key here is to keep the humus content of your soil high. Even when tilth is good, it is important to continue adding humus-building materials. You can never add too much humus to your garden soil.

Fertilizers, on the other hand, should be added thoughtfully, and they are most effectively added in early spring. Add fertilizer before you turn the soil over, to incorporate the nutrients uniformly throughout the soil, at least a couple of weeks prior to planting so they have time to break down. Otherwise, fertilizers can burn tender roots.

CHEMICAL FERTILIZERS: One of the questions most frequently asked of Burpee horticulturists is, "what is the difference between chemical and organic fertilizers?" From the point of view of the plant there is no difference in usability or in the plant's growth. Environmentally, though, there is a big difference. The danger with chemical fertilizers comes from excessive use which can damage your soil by killing beneficial microorganisms and repelling worms, pollute water supplies as excess nitrogen seeps into the water table, and burn plants' roots if the chemical fertilizer comes in contact with them. In addition, chemical fertilizers do nothing to help improve the condition of the soil, whereas organic fertilizers improve the tilth and aeration of the soil.

A complete chemical fertilizer contains the three most important plant nutrients: nitrogen, phosphorus and potassium. Packaged chemical fertilizers identify these nutrients by their percentages of nitrogen (N), phosphorus (P) and potassium (K) or potash in the package. A formula of 5-10-5 garden fertilizer, the most popular all-around formula for vegetable gardens, contains 5% nitrogen, 10% phosphorus, and 5% potassium. The other 80% of the package is inert material

that helps distribute the chemicals evenly.

Nitrogen promotes the rapid growth of green stems and leaves which is why it is especially important for such leaf crops as broccoli, lettuce, and spinach. Nitrogen deficiency causes yellowed leaves and stunted growth, while an excess of nitrogen produces excessive vegetative growth at the expense of the fruit in vine crops, like tomatoes, or root crops, like beets and carrots. Phosphorous stimulates early root formation and is necessary for fruit, flower, and seed formation. A deficiency will show up in purple coloring of the leaves and small and spindly plants. Potassium helps the plants manufacture sugar and starches, as well as aid in their transport throughout the plant. A deficiency will cause dry, discolored leaves and stunted plants.

Don't automatically sprinkle or spread a chemical fertilizer on your garden every spring or fall. You could be doing more harm than good. Here is where a soil test is important. Your test reading may show that you need only one or two nutrients, not a complete fertilizer, in which case you can buy what you need separately, in the quantities you need, at your garden store or nursery.

If you use a chemical fertilizer, make sure it is a slow-release fertilizer. Organic fertilizers are preferred, though. The ideal method is to spread an inch or more of compost over the entire garden every spring or fall, dig it in and let it work for you. Plan to grow crops that are heavy feeders and need large amounts of nitrogen in a location where beans grew the year before. Peas, beans and other legumes, if planted with a legume soil inoculent (see page 67) will release nitrogen into the soil as they grow. After you have harvested the beans, till the vines into the soil to improve its composition and to add nitrogen for next year's leaf crops.

"Side dress" vegetables that need a boost during the growing season by mixing fish emulsion, well-rotted manure, compost, or slow-release fertilizer into the soil around or alongside them. For an organic "side dressing," the amount can be a handful or more. You can't harm the plants with too much organic "side dressing," but with chemical fertilizers it is important to follow the directions carefully. Vine crops like extra fertilizer when the vine begins to run and again when the flower buds are forming. Most other vegetables like it about three weeks after transplanting or when fruit is starting to form.

Here are some sources of organic nutrients:

MANURE: Decomposed cow manure, available commercially bagged in a deodorized form at your local garden center, is a soil-improving humus that supplies nitrogen, phosphorous, and potassium to plants. Humus is an all-important part of the soil, derived from decomposed organic matter rather than minerals. Humus is organic matter in the last stage of decomposition before becoming carbonic acid, ammonia, water, and various trace elements. It is an ingredi-

ent that makes the soil crumbly, soft, and workable—a key to gardening success.

A word of warning: Fresh manure should never be applied to garden plants because it can "burn" them. Apply it in the fall and allow it to break down over the winter, or compost it first and add it to the garden when partially decomposed, but remember that it is not odor-free or weed-free until it is completely decomposed.

The best type of garden manure comes from horses or cows because of its strawy texture and soil-enriching qualities. However, most people are not fortunate enough to have stable manure readily available. Fresh poultry and rabbit manure are usable but they tend to be even more caustic and likely to burn plants. Never use cat or dog manure because, as the animals are meat-eaters, the manure frequently harbors disease or parasites.

BONE MEAL: Bone meal is a slow-acting organic source of phosphorus and limited nitrogen. It is 33 percent phosphorous and 3 percent nitrogen. It must be worked into the soil where the roots of the vegetables can reach it. Bone meal won't burn plant roots.

FISH EMULSION: Fish emulsion supplies nitrogen and some trace elements (elements needed in very small quantities, such as iron, manganese, zinc, and chlorine). Fish meal is 10 percent nitrogen and 6 percent phosphorous.

MULCH: An excellent method

of improving your soil is with a mulch. Mulch means "cover," and this can be grass cuttings, shredded fall leaves, salt hay, wood chips, pine needles, or Agripaper® Natural Mulch material, which is purchased in rolls. All will enrich your garden and add the nutrients your plants constantly need; at the same time, they keep down weeds and hold in moisture.

Plastic mulch traps warmth in the soil, smothers weeds, conserves moisture and protects the developing fruit from damaging ground contact, soil bacteria, and soil insects. It can be lifted in fall and used another season. It's not a difficult task to roll the plastic out on the prepared soil where seeds or seedlings will be planted. Secure the edges with soil, stones, or u-shaped pins made from old coat hangers. To sow the seeds or set out the transplants, use a knife or garden scissors to make a slit in the plastic at the recommended intervals. A bulb planter also makes an excellent tool for cutting the holes for planting. The seed packet will give you proper spacing information.

Mulches of grass clippings, straw, compost, or wood chips are also helpful in conserving moisture and keeping the weeds down. If grass is cut weekly, it doesn't have a chance to go to seed in your mulch pile. Grass piled several inches high creates heat and decomposes quickly; piled too high, it mats down and prevents water from reaching the rest of the pile.

GREEN MANURE: One way farmers improve their soil is

through use of a crop of "green manure." You can, too. After the fall harvest, legume plants are plowed back into the ground to enrich the soil in which they are grown.

The legumes attract soil microbes to the nodules on their roots. These microbes extract nitrogen from the air and convert it to a form usable by the plants. Nitrogen, essential to growing vegetables, gives plants their healthy, green color and helps to produce a maximum crop for harvest. When you plow the plants—stripped of their produce—back under, you provide a source of valuable nitrogen to the next crops grown in that space.

The "green manure" you plow back into the soil provides large amounts of organic material (free of cost) that improve the soil structure, add abundant nutrients that enhance soil fertility, and increase the number of beneficial organisms. The deep root growth of some legumes also helps tap minerals, aerates the soil, and improves drainage. Result: better crops next year.

For the home gardener, beans and peas are the most attractive of all legumes for use as green manure because they offer the bonus of an excellent harvest. Other legumes that can be productively used are alfalfa, clover, and annual vetch, and other green manure crops are barley, wheat, buckwheat, annual rye grass, and oats.

Crop rotation on large farms permits the planting of green manure plants on part of the land each year to revitalize the soil. As a home gardener, you can accomplish the same thing.

Just plant peas and beans in a different place year after year and, after harvesting, till the plants into the soil (remove and discard any plants diseased or infected with insects first).

Green manure crops are ideal contributors to the garden's fertility when the compost pile and other available organic materials are not sufficient for the needs of the garden, especially where the soil is poor. It's a method of composting on a large scale, and the composting takes place over the winter, right where it is needed, giving the crops plenty of time to decompose and work into the top soil.

Compost

With all the environmental concerns about garbage disposal, composting in your own back yard is more important than ever. The compost heap can be a positive step toward recycling Mother Nature's bounty and improving your garden. It is simple. Fall leaves, cut grass, and kitchen vegetable scraps recycled in your garden will improve the texture and nutritional content, and encourage earthworms and beneficial bacteria. Compost breaks down into humus, which reduces the need for fertilizer and water.

Composting can be as simple as a pile of grass cuttings behind the garage or as elaborate as a purchased composter that is attractive enough to sit by the back door. The principle behind composting is to pile the material high, reducing the amount of surface exposed to slow down evaporation. The pile must stay moist to encourage a

plentiful supply of the organisms breaking down the material into rich, garden-ready humus.

Compost is the remains of semidecayed plants. It is the best and cheapest source of organic matter. You can now make compost in your back yard faster and with less mess than Nature can, and the product will be as good or better.

The most important material in a compost pile is not the grass clippings and so forth that are thrown on it, but the millions of microorganisms that must be encouraged to operate in it. Given sufficient levels of moisture, air, and nitrogen, the energy created by these microorganisms will produce heat. Microorganisms decompose the raw materials, resulting in finished compost. Heat is a by-product of the process.

Begin building a compost pile by alternating several layers of vegetable matter with shallow layers of soil. A good-sized pile would be 4 or 5 feet wide and as long as you wish, with a height from 3 to 7 feet. A sprinkle of ground limestone will keep the compost more neutral.

This compost starter bin is easy to make from four 4-foot posts, set in a rectangle, wrapped in chicken wire. If the chicken wire is secured loosely on the fourth side, the bin can be opened easily for removal of compost or for working the compost pile.

Materials to use in your compost: Provided they have not been treated or exposed to chemical weedkillers.

Tree leaves	*Peat moss*
Grass clippings	*Nonwoody mulches*
Weeds (free of seed)	*Animal manures (excluding those of carnivores)*
Straw	
Corn cobs	*Plant trimmings*
Kitchen or table scraps (uncooked vegetable only)	*Vegetable trimmings (beet and turnip tops, pea vines)*

Materials not to use in your compost:

Stones, bones	*Cooked foods, raw meat, or fish that would draw flies and rodents*
Woody branches	
Tomato vines (don't readily decompose)	*Seed-laden tops of weeds*
Diseased plants	*Purslane, crabgrass or lambs-quarters (persistent weeds)*
Animal fats, oily products	

The top of the pile should be slightly concave to catch rain. Do not pack the compost material down.

Turning the compost exposes the particles to the air and helps speed up the process of decomposition. This should be done once or twice a month, when the temperature in the center of the pile reaches approximately 150 degrees Fahrenheit. It isn't really necessary to use a thermometer, because as you turn the compost you will feel the heat as it is released from the pile. Use a pitchfork, turning the outside of the pile to the inside. If the material is dry, sprinkle it with water after turning.

"Curing" takes place as soon as an adequate amount of material has been accumulated. The rate or speed of curing depends on whether the pile has been turned, what the air temperature is, and how much nitrogen is available. If the compost pile has not begun to heat within a month or so, fertilizer or manure should be worked in.

It isn't necessary to cover a compost pile, but you may wish to do so to keep the material from blowing around, to hide the pile, or make it look neater, or to shelter it from too much water during long rainy spells.

Commercial activators can speed the curing process. They usually contain different strains of bacteria that decompose the compost material, in addition to enzymes, hormones, minerals, vitamins, and nitrogen to give the bacteria a boost. Many gardeners simply save some of the previous year's finished compost as "yeast"—about a couple of spadefuls—to add to the new batch, to be sprinkled through the new compost.

THINNING

Thin seedling plants to the distance recommended in the planting guide and on the seed packet, removing the less vigorous plants. Without thinning, you risk stunting the growth of all the plants and ending up with leggy seedlings. Thinning is a nice opportunity to share seedlings with other gardeners, transplant them to another part of the garden, or move some to containers.

For legumes, thin either by carefully hand pulling or snipping unwanted seedlings at the soil line with scissors or pruning shears. This avoids disturbing the shallow roots of the remaining legumes. All other vegetables should be thinned by pulling the "extra" plants carefully out of the ground. The best way to do this is to water the area first, give the moisture time to soak down to the roots, and then gently pull the seedling out at right angles to the remaining plants.

WATERING

Proper watering is essential. Watering correctly conserves water and improves the garden's growth. Roots need both water and air. Too much water can drown the roots and prevent them from breathing, too little can cause leaves to wilt. The best way to test the depth of water penetration is to dig down about 8 inches and see if the moisture has penetrated. Check the day after watering, when water has had time to penetrate. If water is sitting in the bottom of your hole, you know that you have watered too generously and that drainage needs improving.

Watering deeply encourages plant roots to grow deep. Shallow-

Tips for Gardening Success in Drought

- *Mulching conserves moisture, since it slows evaporation from the soil. If dry soil is mulched, it tends to stay dry if rainfall is sparse. The time to mulch is when the soil is moist, even if you are not yet ready to plant.*

- *Shaded soil stays moist longer than soil in partial or full sun, a rule you can use to your advantage.*

- *When plants and rows are closely spaced (so as to overlap only slightly), the soil is shaded. This means that moisture will evaporate from the soil at a slower rate. (It also means that weeds have less chance to take hold in the garden.)*

- *Like all garden plants, weeds require water to thrive. Thus, weeds are competitors for garden water, and many weeds have root structures that give them an edge over your garden plants. Well-rooted plants are better equipped to survive drought than shallow-rooted ones. Weed often, as soon as unwanted plants appear.*

- *It is better to water deeply rather than frequently. Soil-soaking garden hoses are designed to allow water to drip slowly and steadily into the ground. Position the hoses close to the plants you wish to water. Or, remove the nozzle from a conventional garden hose and simply place the hose on the ground, irrigating a section of the garden at a time. Allow water to run until it soaks deeply into the soil. One thorough watering every 10 to 14 days is preferable to more frequent, superficial waterings, and should be sufficient. Water in the early morning or evening, so the heat of the day doesn't evaporate the moisture as quickly.*

- *A windbreak will help slow evaporation. Providing a windbreak can be practical for a small garden in windy areas, providing some relief from moisture loss.*

rooted plants need frequent watering, are more easily disturbed or injured during cultivation, and will bake in the sun on hot days. You must therefore water the soil, not the plants. The best way to accomplish this is to water heavily every four or five days using a drip system that delivers water at low pressure at the soil level. If you water with overhead sprinklers, water early in the day so that the foliage has time to dry off before evening, to minimize disease problems from dampness and cool night temperatures. Daily sprinkling will defeat your purpose, wasting water and leaving you with shallow-rooted plants. A rain gauge, available at garden centers or from mail order catalogs, is a helpful tool for measuring rainfall. One inch of water weekly should be enough for all but the hottest or driest weeks.

Watering should ideally be done early in the morning or in the evening. Those are the times plants absorb water best, and less water will be lost through evaporation. You must keep vegetable plants well-watered during the growing season, and be especially vigilant during dry spells. Keep the soil evenly moist.

A good mulch conserves water by retarding evaporation, retaining the moisture around the plant, and keeping the soil warm and protected from the weeds that compete with the plants for water.

There are a number of watering tools, from a variety of sprinklers to cone and fan sprays. For vegetable garden use, the most practical and the least wasteful of water is the soaker hose. Lay it between rows, holes down, for a deep soaking of the roots, holes up for a fine spray.

TOOLS

Today's gardening tools are a pleasure to use. They are light-weight (the weight is in the tool and not the handle), to make your garden tasks easier.

If you're a container gardener,

your tool needs are simple. All you need are a hand trowel and a watering can fitted with a head pierced with tiny holes, for gentle watering. You could use a dibble too, but this you can improvise from the handle of any old garden tool, or solid stick which has been sharpened to a point.

When gardening outdoors, there are additional tools you will need:

A homemade trellis for climbing vines.

- A cultivator-weeder is two handy tools in one and a good investment for a large vegetable garden. The cultivator side, with three sturdy, pointed prongs, loosens the compacted soil between and around plants. Turn it over and you have a light-weight weeder blade which cuts weeds off at soil level.
- A spade is used for heavy digging. Standard size is 8 inches wide but other widths are available. Choose a size that isn't too heavy for you to manage. Lifting too big a load can deplete your energy quickly.
- Garden line, for laying out straight rows, consists of two sharp stakes connected by heavy string, the length of which must be longer than the rows you plan to sow. This, like the dibble, you can improvise yourself from clothesline, twine, and the like.
- A draw hoe is for cutting out weeds and breaking up crusted earth. The head is about 6 inches wide.
- A garden rake is used for leveling the soil, removing stones and, in some cases, thinning.
- A gardener's knife has many uses including harvesting crops, cutting flowers, pruning and removing diseased parts from plants. It's the handy helper to carry. Buy a good one and keep it sharp.

WINNING THE WEED BATTLE

First to germinate and grow when a garden site is cultivated and the soil loosened up are the native plants, the weeds whose seeds have been lying dormant in the soil. Unfortunately, in the race to feast on soil nutrients and be the first to break ground, cultivated seeds come in second to weeds.

In some areas, gardeners have found a way to get a head start on winning this battle with the weeds. They cultivate and prepare the seed bed a couple of weeks—more, if the season permits—before it's needed to plant seeds. The weeds don't know it's a trick and they germinate quickly. The wily gardener then hoes the weeds away just before sowing his vegetable seeds. The result is a lot fewer weed seeds from one season to the next. The weeds become easier to recognize, isolate, and control—a victory for the vegetable seeds in the struggle for water, nutrients, space, and sun.

During the growing season, hoe shallowly (so as not to disturb roots) and hand-weed close to the plants to keep weeds under control. Control them by frequent cultivation, or use a mulch to keep them from germinating and growing (see page 30).

SUPPORTING AND PRUNING

Growing tomatoes in cages allows free circulation of air, discourages mildew and pests, and keep fruit off the ground and exposed to the sun. You'll enjoy a healthier tomato crop, earlier.

The reasons for supporting plants are many: higher crop yields, cleaner fruit that is free of rot (from lying on wet soil), less damage from pests, and more space for other crops. Supporting such plants as tomatoes, cucumbers, and pole beans can enable you to use garden space more effectively. Supports of all kinds can be either purchased or easily made at home.

Small gardens benefit from growing vertical crops. Crops produce a higher yield earlier because more sun reaches a greater leaf and vegetable surface. Each individual plant grown vertically needs between 3 and 5 square feet of ground whereas sprawling plants can have a 16- to 64-foot spread. An ordinarily unused narrow space along a fence or at the side of a garage is perfect for such vertical plants as peas, beans, squash, tomatoes, sweet potatoes, melons, gourds, and cucumbers.

The supports themselves can be as simple as a forked tree branch or broomstick driven ½ foot into the ground, or as elaborate as a purchased galvanized wire fence, galvanized steel rod tomato tower, or tomato cage.

Season Extenders

Sooner or later every backyard gardener will look for ways of extending the growing season. This is usually done by protecting the plants before and after the last spring frost and after the first frost in the fall. Devices such as cloches, hotkaps, grow tunnels, and cold frames all help you get an early start on your crops. The general purpose of all of these devices is to improve the climate right in your garden by trapping the warmth of the sun during the day and holding it around the plant and soil during the night. The daytime temperature will increase 8 to 10 degrees Fahrenheit, causing the plant to grow faster and escape the dangers of frosts at night. This will roughly double the plant's growth rate. Thus, corn that would have grown 3 inches tall in an uncovered row will shoot up 6 inches under protection.

Although cold frames are an excellent way of raising your plants for transplanting, they will probably be too small for extending all of your spring crops. You will need additional ways of extending directly in the garden. Cloches are usually small devices to cover individual plants, and grow tunnels cover entire rows. The simplest cloche is nothing more than a plastic gallon milk container with the bottom half removed. They can be pushed directly into the soil over the individual plant; plus, they have the added advantage of the cap, which can be removed to keep the plant from overheating.

A cone-shaped cloche 18 inches in diameter or larger can be made with fiberglass-reinforced plastic. It can be purchased or easily made yourself using polyethylene pulled over wooden supports. These larger cloches will give your plants more room to grow.

Grow tunnels are row covers made of lightweight synthetic fabrics. They cover entire rows of vegetables and provide more room than the smaller cloches. Row covers can improve the germination and accelerate growth. The boost from row covers is greatest for heat-loving crops. Four to six weeks into the season, it will be too hot under the covers for most plants, with the exceptions of melons and squash, and the fabric must be removed. But by this time your plants are well on their way. In the fall, the row covers can be replaced and again provide protection against those first few frosts, extending your season. Be careful not to let your plants touch the cover; as frost settles on the fabric it will damage the part of the plant it touches.

Row covers are also an ideal way to control insects. Vegetables that are covered immediately after being sown or transplanted can grow virtually insect-free for as long as 6 weeks with no pesticides. The fabric not only keeps out foliage-eaters, such as the Colorado potato beetle, but also aphids and leaf hoppers that can spread a virus. They keep out loopers, flea beetles, and cucumber beetles, too. The only thing they do not keep out are those insects that winter in the soil. The warmth can bring out the squash-vine borers earlier, and you must keep a vigil so they don't devour your crop. Crop rotation is doubly important if you use row covers.

One word of warning about row covers: Take off the blankets for pollination. You need the bees to pollinate your melons, cucumbers, and squash. Remove them soon after the female plants flower, when all of the plants are in bloom.

When covered with clear plastic, this frame will act as a greenhouse.

VEGETABLE SOWING GUIDE

| VEGETABLE | INDOOR SOWING | | OUTDOOR SOWING |
	TIME NEEDED TO REACH TRANSPLANT SIZE	WHEN TO TRANSPLANT TO THE GARDEN	WHEN TO SOW OUTDOORS
Artichoke, Globe	6–8 weeks	Mid to late spring	After all danger of frost.
Asparagus	6–8 weeks	Mid to late spring	As early as possible in spring.
Beans, Fava		Not recommended	As early as possible in spring.
Beans, Lima	3–4 weeks*	After all danger of frost, when ground is warm	After all danger of frost when ground is warm; continue sowing until midsummer.
Beans, Shell		Not recommended	Sow after all danger of frost when ground is warm; for green shell beans, continue sowing until midsummer.
Beans, Snap		Not recommended	Sow after all danger of frost when ground is warm; continue sowing until midsummer.
Beets		Not recommended	As early in spring as possible; continue sowing until midsummer.
Broccoli	6 weeks	Mid spring; stands some frost.	As early as possible in spring; in early summer for fall crops; in fall in Zones 9 and 10.
Brussels Sprouts	8–10 weeks	Mid spring; stands some frost; mid-summer for fall crops	In early summer for fall crops; in fall in Zones 9 and 10.
Cabbage	6–8 weeks	Mid spring; stands some frost; mid to late summer for fall crops	As early as possible in spring; in early summer for fall crops; in fall in Zones 9 and 10.
Carrots		Not recommended	As early as possible in spring; continue sowing until midsummer; in fall in Zones 9 and 10.
Cauliflower	6–8 weeks	Mid spring; stands some frost; mid to late summer for fall crops	As early as possible in spring; in early summer for fall crops; in fall in Zones 9 and 10.
Celery	10 weeks	Late spring to early summer	After last heavy frost for late summer-to-fall crops.
Chicory, for greens	4–5 weeks*	Mid spring on	As soon as possible in spring; resow every 2 weeks; fall in Zones 9 and 10.

*Optional, but normally direct sown outdoors.
NOTE: Some types of vegetables are best grown from roots, sets, "eyes" or plants. These include: garlic (sets), horseradish (roots), potatoes (eyes), shallots (sets) and sweet potatoes (plants). In addition to growing from seed, onions are often grown from sets or plants; rhubarb from roots.

| VEGETABLE | INDOOR SOWING | | OUTDOOR SOWING |
	TIME NEEDED TO REACH TRANSPLANT SIZE	WHEN TO TRANSPLANT TO THE GARDEN	WHEN TO SOW OUTDOORS
Chicory, for roots		Not recommended	After danger of heavy frost (late spring to early summer). Dig roots in fall for indoor forcing.
Chinese Cabbage	4–5 weeks*	Mid spring; mid to late summer for fall crops	Mid to late summer for fall crops.
Collards	4–5 weeks*	Mid spring; mid to late summer for fall crops	As early as possible in spring; mid to late summer for fall crops.
Corn, Sweet		Not recommended	After all danger of frost when ground is warm; repeat sowing every 7 to 14 days until midsummer.
Cowpeas		Not recommended	After all danger of frost when ground is warm.
Cress, Garden	Sow indoors year-round	Do not transplant; grow indoors	As early as possible in spring; mid to late summer for fall crops; in fall in Zones 9 and 10.
Cucumbers	4 weeks	After all danger of frost	After all danger of frost when ground is warm.
Endive	6–8 weeks	Mid spring; stands some frost	As early as possible in spring; mid to late summer for fall crops; in fall in Zones 9 and 10.
Eggplant	8–10 weeks	After all danger of frost	Not recommended.
Kale	4–5 weeks*	Mid spring; mid to late summer for fall crops	As early as possible in spring; mid to late summer for fall crops.
Kohlrabi	3–4 weeks	Mid through late spring; mid to late summer for fall crops	As early as possible in spring; mid to late summer for fall crops.
Leeks	8–10 weeks	Mid spring	As early as possible in spring; in fall in Zones 9 and 10.
Lettuce, Head	8–10 weeks	Mid spring; stands some frost	As early as possible in spring; mid to late summer for fall crops; in fall in Zones 9 and 10.
Lettuce, Loosehead	4 weeks*	Mid spring; late summer for fall crops	As early as possible in spring; continue sowing every 2 weeks in spring; mid to late summer for fall crops.

VEGETABLE	INDOOR SOWING		OUTDOOR SOWING
	TIME NEEDED TO REACH TRANSPLANT SIZE	WHEN TO TRANSPLANT TO THE GARDEN	WHEN TO SOW OUTDOORS
Melons (Cantaloupe, Muskmelon, Watermelon)	3–4 weeks	After all danger of frost	After all danger of frost when ground is warm.
Mustard Greens	3–4 weeks*	Mid spring; late summer for fall crops	As early as possible in spring; mid to late summer for fall crops; in fall in Zones 9 and 10.
Okra	4 weeks*	Late spring	After all danger of frost when ground is warm.
Onions	6–10 weeks	Mid spring; stands some frost	As early as possible in spring.
Pak Choi	4 weeks*	Mid spring; mid to late summer for fall crops	As early as possible in spring; mid to late summer for fall crops; in fall in Zones 9 and 10.
Parsnips		Not recommended	After danger of heavy frost.
Peas		Not recommended	As early as possible in spring; mid to late summer for fall crops.
Peppers	8–10 weeks	After all danger of frost	Not recommended.
Pumpkins	4 weeks	After all danger of frost	After all danger of frost when ground is warm.
Radishes		Not recommended	As early as possible in spring; mid to late summer for fall crops; in fall in Zones 9 and 10.
Rhubarb	6–8 weeks	Mid spring on	As soon as the ground can be worked in spring.
Roquette	3–4 weeks*	Mid spring on	After all danger of frost.
Rutabaga		Not recommended	As soon as ground can be worked in spring; resow in midsummer for fall crops.
Spinach	4 weeks*		As early as possible in spring; mid to late summer for fall crops.
Spinach, Malabar	4–5 weeks*	Late spring on	After all danger of frost; early spring or late summer; fall in Zones 9 and 10.
Squash, Summer	4 weeks*	After all danger of frost	After all danger of frost when ground is warm.
Squash, Winter	4 weeks*	After all danger of frost	After all danger of frost when ground is warm.

*Optional, but normally direct sown outdoors.
NOTE: Some types of vegetables are best grown from roots, sets, "eyes" or plants. These include: garlic (sets), horseradish (roots), potatoes (eyes), shallots (sets) and sweet potatoes (plants). In addition to growing from seed, onions are often grown from sets or plants; rhubarb from roots.

| Vegetable | Indoor Sowing | | Outdoor Sowing |
	Time Needed to Reach Transplant Size	When to Transplant to the Garden	When to Sow Outdoors
Swiss Chard	4–6 weeks*	Mid spring to midsummer	As early as possible in spring; continue sowing until midsummer.
Tomatoes	6–8 weeks	After all danger of frost	Fast-maturing standard varieties can be sown after danger of heavy frost or when ground is fairly warm. Otherwise, not recommended.
Turnips		Not recommended	As early as possible in spring; mid to late summer for fall crops; in fall in Zones 9 and 10.

There are even elaborate wooden pyramids. A fence of any kind makes a perfect support; stretch nylon mesh netting tightly between two poles at either end of the garden for vines to grow up. Or put several branches or bamboo poles together to grow vines in a teepee arrangement. If the teepee is covered with netting, the plants will grow all over it.

Stakes

Anchor sturdy stakes at least 12 inches in the ground. Set plants about 6 inches from the stakes. As the plants grow, allow only one or two main stems to develop per plant. Pinch out any other side shoots as they form so the plants will grow tall. Gently tie the one or two shoots to the stake when they are 1½ to 2 feet tall; don't pull them tightly. Give them room to grow comfortably.

Tomato Cages

This is my favorite method of staking tomatoes. Cages are easy to store and last indefinitely. You can buy tomato cages (40 inches tall) or make them with reinforced galvanized wire mesh;

5½ linear feet of 6-inch-square mesh 40 or more inches wide will make an 18-inch-diameter cylinder of good height. Secure cages to stakes to prevent toppling over. Place each cage around a single plant; the shoots will grow and enlarge within the cage. As the plants grow taller, a second cage can easily be stacked on top of the first. There is no need to prune or tie up plants. They will grow through the squares of mesh and pull themselves up.

Tomato cages encourage good air circulation, discourage mildew and pests. Try growing several pea or bean seedlings around the outside of a larger cage, tying them lightly to the cage as they grow, and use the inside of the cage as a compost feeder by filling it with compost. You can protect seedlings from wind and create a warm microclimate by placing black plastic around the cage for the first few weeks.

Poles

For pole beans, 10-foot poles should be placed from 2 to 3 feet apart and buried to a depth of about 2 feet. You can form a tripod, like an Indian teepee,

using three poles or fairly straight tree branches placed 3 to 4 feet apart at the base and tied together at the top.

Trellis

Sink several strong posts at 6-foot intervals, then attach trellis netting of durable, reusable white nylon, or stretch two or more strong wires across the posts, with one strand near the top of the post and one strand 8 to 12 inches above the ground. Plant between the posts, close to the netting, spacing the plants 1½ to 2½ feet apart. Prune to one or two shoots per plant.

As the plants grow, weave the stems into the netting. Or you can cut a long strand of strong, weather-resistant twine for each shoot, fasten it to the bottom wire and then wrap the twine loosely around the lower stems of the plants and tie the other end to the top wire. Keep wrapping the twine loosely around the stems as the plants grow.

Portable, folding A-frame trellises are available ready-made or can be built using two wooden frames, 5 feet by 6 feet, hinged at the top and covered with chicken wire.

PLANT PORTRAITS

The choices of what to grow in a vegetable garden are limited only by your taste and preferences. We have listed more than sixty of the most popular vegetables from the Burpee catalogs here, but they are only a beginning. Some categories, tomatoes and lettuce, for example, hold many more varieties than we could list. Every year brings new hybrids and breakthroughs in disease-resistant varieties. Gardening magazines and gardening columns in periodicals will help keep you up-to-date on the latest plant developments.

The information we offer in this section is meant to save you the inconvenience of learning by trial and error. The back of any seed packet has all the information you need for planting that particular variety—and you won't find that information repeated here—but we want to give you a broader foundation of gardening information, to help you be a more successful gardener and to give you the information you need to make your decisions about what to grow.

The vegetables are arranged in alphabetical order by their common name. If the vegetable has more than one name, it has been cross-referenced to make it easier to find. Different varieties of the same vegetable are listed under the vegetable names, not by variety name. For example, cantaloupe is listed under "melon," and Buttercrunch lettuce is listed under "lettuce."

Every entry explains the ease of growing that vegetable whether it be easy, moderate, or difficult. The days (or, rarely, years) to harvest are approximate, and are listed to help you plan your garden. Days to harvest followed by an asterisk (*) are average times from setting out indoor-started plants until the first fruits mature. The time it will take any plant to reach maturity varies with your location and the weather; don't try to set your calendar strictly by these dates.

The average hours of sun needed per day is indicated by symbols. The first symbol is what the vegetable prefers, but the plant is adaptable to all conditions listed.

○ *Sun*—Six hours or more of direct sunlight per day.

◑ *Part Shade*—Three to six hours of direct sunlight per day.

In many cases we have listed the family that each vegetable belongs to so you can understand the similarities of vegetables of the same family, and to help you rotate families as well as specific vegetable crops in order to keep pests and diseases from spreading. Only the ten largest families are identified. Where a family name is not given, the vegetable is the only member of its family commonly grown in American vegetable gardens.

The days to germination predict when each type of seed will germinate, so you'll know when to look for new seedlings. If growing them indoors, it will help you know when to move them to a sunny window.

Both the growth temperature and the temperature for germination are given to help you understand an individual seed's needs.

The challenges, adventures, and joy of the garden all are waiting for you to begin. Happy gardening!

The fruits of the harvest

PLANTING GUIDE FOR LEAFY GREENS

TYPE	SEED PLANTING DEPTH (INCHES)	SPACING OF THINNED PLANTS (INCHES)	SPACING OF ROWS	DAYS TO MATURITY	PKT. SOWS X FEET OF ROW	APPROXIMATE YIELD PER 10-FOOT ROW
Lettuce, Looseleaf	½	4–6	1½'	45–50	1 Pkt. = 30'	5 lbs.
Lettuce, Crisphead	½	12" or more	1–1½'	80–90	1 Pkt. = 30'	10 heads
Lettuce, Butterhead	½	6–12	1½'	75–80	1 Pkt. = 30'	10–20 heads
Lettuce, Cos	½	6–12	1½'	83	1 Pkt. = 30'	10 heads
Chicory, Sugarhat	½	6–12	1½'	86	1 Pkt. = 30'	10–20 heads
Collards	¼–½	12–18	3'	60	1 Pkt. = 40'	10 lbs.
Garden Cress	¼	—	1'	10	1 Pkt. = 20'	3–5 lbs.
Watercress	¼	—	—	50	—	—
Endive	½	12	1½' or more	90	1 Pkt. = 20'	10 heads
Kale	¼	12	2'	55–65	1 Pkt. = 30'	10 lbs.
Mustard Greens	¼	5	12–18	35–40	1 Pkt. = 50'	7–10 plants
Garden Rocket	¼	6	15"	35	1 Pkt. = 30'	5 lbs.
Spinach	½	5–6	1½'	42–50	1 Pkt. = 30'	5–10 lbs.
Swiss Chard	½	8–10	18"	50–60	1 Pkt. = 25'	10 lbs.
Celery	¼	4–6	1½–2'	105–103	1 Pkt. = 100 plts.	20–30 plants

Artichoke 'Green Globe'

Artichoke (Globe Artichoke) Sunflower Family Difficult ○
Days to Harvest: 100
Days to Germinate: 14 to 21
Temperature to Germinate: 70 to 75 degrees Fahrenheit
Growth Temperature: 60 to 70 degrees Fahrenheit
Height: 3 to 4 feet
Characteristics: It is the edible flower buds that we harvest. Most often grown as a perennial in mild-winter areas like Castroville, California ("Artichoke Capital of the World"), artichokes can be enjoyed by any gardener with at least 100 frost-free days, if grown in containers to bring indoors for winter protection. Well-mulched plants can withstand 20-degree Fahrenheit temperatures. Keep well-watered during dry spells or they will go dormant. Harvest in fall if grown as an annual, fall and spring in mild climates. 'Green Globe' is a good variety for the home gardener.
Cultural Information: Artichokes like a fertile, loamy soil. If your soil is heavy, work in compost and manure. Manure is also an excellent source of nitrogen, needed for good growth and larger, more tender artichokes. Direct sow about two weeks before last frost. It is important to protect artichokes from low temperatures. Keep seed bed evenly moist. Mulch well after plants are established. Artichokes are nearly problem-free, but watch for aphids and rabbits; to prevent crown rot, don't allow soil to become waterlogged.
Harvest: Ready when unopened buds are the size of oranges and gray-green in color (fall

crops are tipped with purple). Cut the stem 1 to 2 inches below the bud.

Arugula; see *Garden rocket*

Asparagus Lily Family Easy ○

Years to Harvest: from crowns, 2; from seed, 3
Days to Germinate: 7 to 14
Temperature to Germinate: 68 to 86 degrees Fahrenheit
Growth Temperature: 60 to 70 degrees Fahrenheit
Height: 3 to 7 feet
Characteristics: Because asparagus need to go dormant for winter, they don't thrive in the southernmost United States. They are grown commercially in southern California where, when cut back in fall, they will go dormant. Asparagus are perennials that give ten to twenty years—or longer—of harvest. (We know of one bed in England still producing after 118 years.) Asparagus can be grown from seed or from crowns (roots). One- and two-year-old crowns, which can be purchased through catalogs or garden centers, are easier. Harvest asparagus in its third year. Planting should be done in the spring.

Asparagus are excellent raw, sliced into cold salads; if cooked, boil or steam only until tender, 5 to 10 minutes. Homegrown asparagus are much more flavorful. The fernlike foliage makes an attractive green background for a flower planting.
Cultural Information: Asparagus beds need more preparation initially than other vegetable beds, but are a cinch to maintain once established. The key to success is adding enough

organic matter to maintain a pH of 6.5 to 6.8, providing good drainage and controlling weeds.

A row 50 feet long will feed an average family of four. To plant from seed, follow the directions on the seed packet. To plant crowns, dig a trench approximately 12 inches wide and 15 inches deep. Add six inches of organic matter; well-rotted manure is best, but compost or peat moss will do. Water well to settle, then mound the soil a few inches in the center of the trench. Mix one part organic matter (manure if available) to two parts of the original soil from the trench, adding superphosphate at the rate of 5 lbs per 100 feet. Soak the crowns for a few hours in warm water to give them a drink before planting. (Sown from seed, asparagus roots are usually large enough for transplanting after 1 year.) Set the fragile crowns in the prepared trench, 18 inches apart; place the crowns on the apex of the mound, and gently fan the roots down the side. Press gently into place. Cover with 2 inches of the soil-compost mix and water again. Over the summer, continue to add soil, an inch or two at a time, to cover the stems as they appear, until the trench is filled and level with the ground. Twice during the growing season, carefully side dress each plant with a handful of 10–10–10 slow-release fertilizer. For white asparagus, hill the soil around the spears 8 to 10 inches and harvest when the tips come through the top of the hill.

Unchecked weeds can dominate the bed in the early years

and suffocate the young plants. When the trench is filled to ground level, mulch with 4 to 6 inches of organic matter to control weeds and feed the asparagus roots. Choose rust-resistant varieties like 'Mary Washington' and 'Jersey Giant'. The asparagus beetle is a common pest throughout North America. Clean up garden debris in the fall, as the beetle hibernates for the winter in plant refuse. Plant asparagus near tomatoes; asparagus repel the nematodes that plague tomatoes, and tomatoes repel the asparagus beetle. Ladybugs and trichogramma wasps prey on the beetle and should be encouraged. Anthracnose is the most common and serious asparagus disease.
Harvest: At harvest they may be anywhere from the diameter of a pencil to ½-inch thick (less tender, but perfect for soup).

Beans Pea Family ○

For specific growing information, see the "Legume Planting Guide," page 45.
General Characteristics: Beans can be grouped according to their usage as snap (or string), shell, and dried. They can then be further divided within each group by their habit (*e.g.*, bush or pole) and again by color (*e.g.*, yellow bush snap beans or green bush snap beans). We have listed them alphabetically by the best-known member of each group and have cross referenced the other names. If one type of bean, Limas for example, can be grown as a bush or a pole variety, we explain what that involves. Pole beans are so named because they wind them-

Asparagus 'Jersey Giant'

selves around supports or poles as they climb. Often, they need a little guidance in the early stages; gently pick the vines up and set them on the support. Pole beans begin to bear later than bush beans, but yield more heavily over a longer period and some produce larger pods. We have listed different kinds of beans, their characteristics and where they differ from other beans of their type. Cultural information is listed only where it differs from the general cultural information for beans.

A great number of varieties are original to the Americas. Beans are a staple of vegetarian diets, being high in protein, vitamins, fiber, and minerals.

General Cultural Information: When growing beans, prepare your garden soil well as you do for other vegetables. Plant pole beans at the north end of the garden, so that they don't shade smaller plants. Set the supports for pole beans in place before planting the seeds, so you won't risk damage to the plants or their roots (see page 39 for instructions). Because beans attract their own source of nitrogen, they need less nitrogen fertilizer during growth than most vegetables. Excessive application of manure or other fertilizers high in nitrogen will stimulate growth but reduce yields. Remember, beans put nitrogen back in the soil and should be rotated where lettuces, squashes and members of the mustard family have been grown the year before as they lower the nitrogen content of the soil. At season's end, till or dig in the bean stalks to further improve your soil as they decompose over the winter.

Different varieties of beans can be grown side by side, since all beans are self-pollinating.

Beans, with the single exception of favas, must be planted in spring after all danger of frost and after the soil has become warm. If sown in cool soil, bean seeds are very susceptible to rot. Use a garden blanket or a floating row cover to help hold the heat and keep the soil warm. Good bean growth requires nitrogen-fixing bacteria in the soil, so the use of a legume inoculant like Burpee Booster for Peas and Beans, sprinkled in the furrow as you sow, is essential. Beans have shallow root systems, and too-close cultivation can damage them. Cultivate thoroughly for weed control before planting, and once good growth is underway, maintain a four-inch layer of organic mulch.

For specific instructions on timing, spacing, and growing legume seeds, refer to the "Legume Planting Guide" that follows. Beans generally do not transplant well and should be sown where they are to grow, or started in peat pots where transplanting is usually successful and ensures an early harvest.

Common pests include aphids, beetles, and leafhoppers. Common diseases include anthracnose, powdery mildew, and root rot.

Blackeye pea; see *Cowpea*

Broad beans, English; see *Fava beans*

Butter beans; see *Limas*

Chick Peas (Garbanzo Beans, Gram Beans)
Characteristics: Botanically, chick peas are neither true beans nor peas but thrive under the same growing conditions. They have a unique chestnutlike flavor and are usually dried. Chick peas are a popular addition to salads, and can be served on their own as a vegetable or in soup. The plants are bushy, about two feet tall with fernlike foliage. The puffy pods contain one to three beans each.
Cultural Information: Chick peas grow best in a warm climate; other than that, their cultural information is the same as for Bush Limas.
Harvest: Allow pods to dry before they are opened. Store chick peas in an airtight container.

Cowpea (Blackeye Pea, Southern Pea, Crowder Pea)
Characteristics: Southern favorites, but gardeners in other areas should try them too, as they are flavorful and nutritious. There are three types of cowpeas, all easily identified. Blackeye peas produce seeds that have black "eyes." Cream peas have cream-colored seeds and crowder peas bear pods with tightly packed (crowded) peas. 'California Blackeye' is a recommended variety with pods 7 to 8 inches long, well filled with large, smooth-skinned seeds, delicious fresh or dried. Heavy-yielding vines are resistant to wilt, nematodes, and other pea diseases. 'Purple Hull' is one of the most popular southern peas, producing a heavy crop of pods containing white peas with small purple eyes.
Cultural Information: Cowpeas like the same growing conditions as lima beans. They are extremely resistant to heat and

LEGUME PLANTING GUIDE

Variety	Grade of Difficulty	When to Sow	Seed Planting Depth	Spacing Between Seeds (Inches)	Spacing Between Rows (Feet)	Thin To (Inches)	Temperature to Germinate (Fahrenheit)	Days to Germinate	Growth Temperature	Height	Days to Harvest	Seed Required for 100' Row (Pounds)	Approx. Edible Yield for 100' Row[1] (Pounds)
BEANS, BUSH													
Chick peas	easy	After all danger of frost	2	2–3	2–3	4–6	68–80°	7–14	70–80°	2'	100–105	½	20–30 shelled
Fava Beans	easy	As early as possible in spring	2	2–3	2–3	4–6	68–86°	14–21	70°	2–4'	80–90	¾	50 shelled
Limas	easy	After all danger of frost	2	3–4	2½–3½	6–10	68–86°	7–14	70–80°	14–20"	60–80	¾	30–40 shelled
Mung Beans	easy	After all danger of frost	1	2–3	2–3	4–6	65–85°	7–14	70–80°	1–2-½'	90	¼	20–30 shelled
Shell Beans	easy	After all danger of frost	2	2–3	1½–2½	4–6	68–86°	7–14	70–80°	20–22"	65–100	½	20–30 shelled
Snap Beans	easy	After all danger of frost	2	2–3	1½–2½	4–6	68–86°	7–14	70–80°	15–20"	45–60	½	120
BEANS, POLE													
Limas	easy	After all danger of frost	2	3–5 or 8–10 per pole	Poles 2–3 apart	6–10 or 3–4 per pole	68–86°	7–14	70–80°	10–12'	75–95	1½ (100 poles)	50 shelled
Snap Beans	easy	After all danger of frost	2	3–5 or 8–10 per pole	Poles 2–3 apart	6–10 or 3–4 per pole	68–86°	7–14	70–80°	5–8'	60–70	½ (60 poles)	150
PEAS													
Green Peas, Edible-podded Peas, and Snap Peas	easy	As early as possible in spring; or late summer	1–2	1–2	Double, rows 3" apart & 2½' between double rows[2]	1–2	68°	7–14	65–70°	15–16'	55–80	1	20[3]
COW PEAS	easy	After all danger of frost	1½	1½	2–3	12	68–86°	10–14	70–80°	2–2½'	65–80	½	40

[1]Frequent harvesting increases yield.
[2]See text for other growing methods.
[3]Much higher for Snap Peas.

drought, yet too much moisture will reduce the yield. In general, bush-type cowpeas are preferred in northern climates because of the shorter growing season; they are faster to mature than pole beans. In the South, make three successive plantings every three weeks until midsummer for an extended harvest.

Harvest: Immature pods can be harvested and used like snap beans. Cowpeas can be allowed to grow to the green shell or dry stage. Pick green shell beans when the deep green pod color changes to light-yellow, red, purple, or silver, depending on the variety and as explained on the seed packet. For dry peas, leave the pods on the plant until fully mature, then harvest, dry, shell, and treat as described in "Drying Peas and Beans," page 67.

Crowder pea; see *Cowpea*

Fava Beans (English Broad Beans, Windsor Beans, Horse Beans)
Characteristics: Fava beans are a good substitute for lima beans where the growing season is short and cool. The erect, bush-type plants produce pods 7 inches long which contain five to seven flat, oblong beans. Dried fava beans are second to soybeans in protein; fresh green ones have 10 times the protein of snap beans.
Cultural Information: Plant seeds with the "eyes" down to encourage faster rooting.
Harvest: Favas can be picked when green or allowed to dry on the vine. For dry beans, pick pods that seem perfectly dry, let them air-dry a few days longer, then store as you would any other dried bean. (NOTE: Some people of Mediterranean descent have a genetic trait which causes a severe allergic reaction to fava beans.)

Filet beans; see *Chick peas*

Garbanzo beans; see *Chick peas*

Garden beans; see *Snap beans*

Gram beans; see *Chick peas*

Green beans; see *Snap beans*

Haricots Verts (Filet Beans)
Characteristics: These famous green bush snap beans of France are crunchy, rather than fleshy. The slender, shapely pods have wonderful, vibrant flavor. An heirloom (unchanged by plant breeders) variety, 'Triumph de Farcy' bears early and very

Lima Bean
'Fordhook® No. 242'

heavily. 'Vernandon', a variety with good disease resistance, matures in 55 days.
Harvest: Haricots verts must be picked daily when very young —from little "matchsticks" 3 inches long up to 6-inch pencils—and always while still flat before they swell to ¼ inch wide, when they become tough.

Horse beans; see *Fava beans*

Horticultural beans; see *Shell beans*

Kidney beans; see *Shell beans*

Limas (Butter Beans)
Characteristics: Bush types mature earlier than pole limas and do not need support. The varieties vary in shape and size: large thick (Burpee's 'Fordhook'); small thick "potato" type ('Baby Fordhook'); large flat (Burpee's 'Improved'); small flat baby butter lima ('Henderson Bush'). Varieties designated "baby" produce earlier and smaller beans.
Cultural Information: Lima beans are very sensitive to cool, wet conditions and mature more slowly than snap beans. To encourage faster rooting, sow the seeds with the "eyes" down. Limas need especially warm soil temperatures, about 65 degrees Fahrenheit, for good germination, but they like cool growth temperatures. Their flowers drop in high (80 degrees Fahrenheit and above) temperatures.
Like snap beans, limas grow in self-supported bush form or as climbing beans. Pole types produce greater yields over a longer period. The climbing vines should be supported. Space

poles 2 to 3 feet apart and grow several plants around each; or, grow on a bean tower.
In hot climates, baby limas set their pods better and produce earlier than the large seeded varieties. 'Christmas Lima' and 'Florida Speckled Butter' are good for withstanding heat and drought.
Harvest: Limas should be harvested when the seeds are plump and succulent (some baby limas are creamy white when ready.) To keep the plants productive, harvest often.

Mung Beans
Characteristics: Mung beans are eaten primarily as sprouts. They are both delicious and nourishing raw, in salads, or cooked in stir-fried dishes. The beans may also be cooked as for dry shell beans. The bush-type plants are 1 to 2½ feet tall. Pods are held at or above foliage, which makes harvesting easy.
Cultural Information: They have the same cultural requirements as lima beans.
Harvest: Harvest mature pods individually or pull the plants and hang them to dry in a warm, dry, well-ventilated place. Dried pods should be handled with care as they shatter quite easily.

Pinto beans; see *Shell beans*

Shell Beans (Pinto Beans, Kidney Beans, Horticultural Beans)
Characteristics: Shell beans are high in protein and combine with grains to supply a complete protein diet that can be a healthy substitute for meat. Horticultural beans produce green pods flecked with red and can be used as snap beans when picked young; use older beans

as dry beans. Pinto and kidney beans are grown mostly for dry beans (the pinto is best known in "refried bean" dishes). All of these shell beans are bush types and can be grown like bush snap beans.

Harvest: Usually, bush shell beans are harvested as green shell beans when the pods change from green to yellow; at this stage the seeds are fully grown, but not hard and dry. To reach this stage, the plants take about 65 days. The pods can also be allowed to mature fully for use as dry beans; pick when pods are paper-dry.

Snap Beans (Green Beans, Wax Beans, Yellow Beans, Garden Beans, String Beans)

Characteristics: The name "string bean" has fallen out of favor since so many good varieties have been bred with stringless pods. Snap beans with golden-yellow pods are also called wax beans or just plain yellow beans. Our favorite yellow bean for fresh use is 'Brittle Wax'. There are also purple beans, like 'Royal Burgundy'; the pods turn dark-green during cooking. Italian (Romano) beans, like 'Roma II', are wider and flatter, have a rich flavor and are outstanding for freezing.

Pole beans begin to bear later than bush beans, but yield more heavily over a longer period and some produce larger pods. The young pods are delicious both fresh and frozen. 'Burpee Golden' has wide, flat, stringless butter-yellow pods, 5½ to 6½ inches long. The plant starts to grow like a bush bean and sets pods very early, quite close to the ground; then, runners shoot up and continue to bear tender

pods. 'Kentucky Wonder' is a traditional favorite, noted for the distinctive, tasty flavor of both fresh pods and dried light brown seeds (as shell beans). 'Scarlet Runner' is frequently grown on fences where, all summer long, the bright red flowers can be seen and the green pods picked. The pods hold bright scarlet beans.

Cultural Information: You can grow snap beans as bush-type or pole-type plants. Pole beans take longer to mature (about 65 days versus 50 days for bush beans) but are more prolific and are considered by some to be more flavorful. For continuous harvest, plant successive crops of bush beans every two weeks; a single planting of pole beans will continue bearing for a long season. Due to their upright habits, bush beans are easy to cultivate and harvest.

Pole beans climb 5 to 8 feet and should be supported. Bean towers are easy to set up and a space saver. Or, grow in rows on a fence, trellis or netting; thin plants to 6 to 10 inches apart. During excessive heat and dry weather, plants may drop flowers or pods, a condition that will correct itself when the weather improves.

Harvest: Snap beans should be harvested regularly to hasten the growth of more beans, as harvesting stimulates the production of new blossoms and pods. To harvest, hold the stem with one hand while picking the pods off carefully with the other. Harvesting should be done in the morning when evening's dampness has disappeared. The pods should be harvested when still tender, just when the seeds inside the pod have begun to fill

out. At this stage they will snap readily. If the pods are left to grow until they are older, with larger seeds, they will seem more tender if they are French cut (sliced lengthwise in strips) before cooking. Like most vegetables, snap beans have the best flavor when eaten soon after picking. Most varieties are good for canning and pickling, and some are excellent for freezing.

String beans; see *Snap beans*

Wax beans; see *Snap beans*

Windsor beans; see *Fava beans*

Yellow beans; see *Snap beans*

Beets Goosefoot Family Easy ○

Days to Harvest: 45 to 65
Days to Germinate: 3 to 14 at most
Temperature to Germinate: 68 to 85 degrees Fahrenheit
Growth Temperature: 80 degrees Fahrenheit
Height: 8 inches

Characteristics: The beet is a sweet, colorful, delicious vegetable that does well in cool weather. You can enjoy fresh beets twice in a season by planting early spring and again in late summer. The tops of beets are delicious and a wonderful source of vitamins; they can be eaten raw in salads, or cooked and served like spinach. You can choose from many different types of beets. Enjoy them when roots are half-grown or when they reach full size. Beets attain their peak of sweet flavor baked, or brushed with oil and grilled for 40 to 45 minutes.

Bush Bean 'Burpee's Stringless Green Pod'

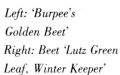

Left: 'Burpee's Golden Beet'
Right: Beet 'Lutz Green Leaf, Winter Keeper'

Burpee's 'Golden Beet' is a favorite both for color and outstanding flavor. The handsome, golden roots are excellent in salads, gourmet borscht, or pickled. Best when eaten small, but they don't become fibrous or lose their sweet flavor when mature. As a bonus, they will not "bleed." Although easy to grow, germination rate is lower than for other beets; sow seeds thickly. 'Cylindra' is a unique, long, cylindrical beet that will give three to four times the number of uniform slices as a round beet. 'Little Ball' is smaller, dark red, very sweet and tender—good for pickling. As a small-topped variety, it is good for wide row planting.

Cultural Information: Because beets like cool weather, they can be planted in early spring when they also benefit from the abundance of rain. You can plant a second crop in late summer, but provide adequate water during this sometimes-dry season. Beets love humus and thrive with a pH of approximately 7.0. To guarantee a successful harvest they will need phosphorus and potassium. It is important to add several inches of well-rotted manure or a slow-release 5–10–10 fertilizer to the soil before planting. CAUTION: Manure must be aged sufficiently or your root crop will be poorly developed.

Soak seeds in lukewarm water well before planting (overnight is ideal) to ensure even germination. A good garden trick is to plant quick-to-germinate radish seed directly above beet seed. The emerging radishes will mark the row, develop above the beets, and be harvested without interfering with the growth of the beets; gardeners benefit from two crops in a single wide row. Plant beet seeds ½ inch deep and 1 inch apart; cover with ¾ inch fine soil. Thin to 2 inches apart after two weeks, then thin again for a final spacing approximately 4 inches apart. (Each beet seed is actually dry fruit containing up to 8 seeds. This is why seedlings must be thinned to ensure enough space between plants for proper development.) It is important to keep the area weeded and watered. Beets need weekly watering. They develop rings and can crack if dry spells alternate with wet spells.

Harvest: Harvest when roots are 2 to 5 inches in diameter and before the first hard frost. Remove tops with sharp knife, leaving about ½ inch of leaf stem attached to the root. Beets can be frozen or canned, but it is easy to store them under cool, moist conditions. Roots for storage should be 2 to 5 inches in diameter. Refrigerate for 5 to 7 months with high humidity. To maintain this humidity, place roots in plastic bags with perforations and cover with damp sawdust, peat moss or sand. Or, store in a root cellar at 32 to 40 degrees Fahrenheit.

Beet, spinach; see *Swiss chard*

Blackeye pea; see *Beans, Cowpea*

Broccoli Mustard Family
Easy ○
Days to Harvest: 55 to 85*
Days to Germinate: 3 to 10
Temperature to Germinate: 70 to 80 degrees Fahrenheit
Growth Temperature: 65 to 75 degrees Fahrenheit
Height: 2 to 3 feet
Characteristics: One of the more nutritious vegetables, broccoli has large amounts of vitamins A and C and significant amounts of vitamin B, iron, and protein. Delicious raw with a dip or cooked just to the point of tenderness, broccoli heads are composed of tiny, tight, blue-green flower buds in clusters on compact stalks.

There are two types of variety. One, such as 'Premium Crop Hybrid', produces a single large head. The other, as in 'Green Goliath' and 'Bonanza Hybrid', produces a slightly smaller head and many side shoots that develop later and extend the harvest.

Cultural Information: Broccoli thrive in cool weather; most will even take a light frost, but take precautions if heavy frost is expected. For an early harvest start seeds indoors approximately 5 to 6 weeks before the last spring frost. Seedlings can be transplanted into the garden three weeks before last spring frost. Broccoli need phosphorus and potassium, easily provided with slow-release 5–10–10 fertilizer applied just before planting. Generous applications of wood ash provide phosphorous. Rotate broccoli yearly to avoid depleting the soil and carryover pest and disease problems. Mulch around the plants will help to conserve moisture and keep the roots cool during hot spells. To avoid spotting and rot, don't water from overhead. The most common broccoli pests are the cutworm and the cabbage worm. (See "Planting Guide for Cole Crops," below.)

Harvest: Harvest when fully enlarged but before the flower buds begin to open. Trim the stems 6 to 7 inches below the heads. With the sprouting types, harvest the central stalk but allow the smaller shoots to continue

to develop over several weeks. Be sure to soak harvested broccoli in warm water with a little vinegar and salt for a few minutes to remove many of the tiny insects (minute larvae and aphids) that broccoli attracts.

Brussels Sprouts Mustard Family Easy ○

Days to Harvest: 90 to 100* (Early type 60 to 70*; Mid-Season 72 to 85*; Winter 105*)
Days to Germinate: 3 to 10
Temperature to Germinate: 68 to 86 degrees Fahrenheit
Growth Temperature: 60 to 70 degrees Fahrenheit
Height: 3 feet
Characteristics: These plants grow erect with tiny "cabbages" (sprouts) forming along the stem at each leaf. Brussels sprouts should be grown as a fall crop, because a touch of fall frost improves the flavor. They can be sown in spring or early summer directly into the garden, or started in a cold frame. Brussels sprouts love cool weather and can be enjoyed well into

the winter months. Delicious when steamed or boiled just to the point of tenderness and served with butter. 'Jade Cross E Hybrid' is a recommended variety with large, firm, closely set, blue-green sprouts excellent for eating fresh or freezing. 'Oliver' is good for areas with a short growing season.

Cultural Information: Work well-rotted manure or a slow-release 5–10–10 fertilizer into the soil before planting. Side dress each plant monthly with approximately 2 teaspoons fertilizer or compost and manure. Mature plants should stand approxi-

Above: Broccoli 'Bonanza Hybrid'
Below: Brussels Sprouts

PLANTING GUIDE FOR COLE CROPS

CROP	SEED PLANTING DEPTH (INCHES)	SPACING OF THINNED PLANTS (INCHES)	SPACING OF ROWS (FEET)	APPROXIMATE DAYS TO MATURITY	APPROXIMATE NUMBER OF PLANTS PER PACKET
Broccoli	¼–½	15 or more	2½–3	55–58*	50
Brussels sprouts	¼–½	24	2½–3	90–95*	50 (hybrids) 125 (standard)
Cabbage Early	¼–½	12–18	2½	60–70*	50
Midseason and Late	¼–½	18–24	2½–3	72–105*	50
Cauliflower	¼–½	18–24	2½	52–85*	50
Chinese Cabbage	¼–½	8–12	2	62–75*	50

*From date plants are set out in garden.

mately 15 to 20 inches apart in rows 24 to 30 inches wide. Mulch will help retain moisture, especially during hot, dry weather. Many gardeners break off the lower branches at the bottom 6 to 8 inches of the stem to encourage early sprouts to grow faster, and the plant to grow taller and thus produce more sprouts. If you want all of your sprouts to mature at the same time, cut the top 6 inches of the plant a month before anticipated harvest. If you leave the top on, you can harvest—from the bottom up—over a longer period of time. (See "Planting Guide for Cole Crops," page 49.)

Harvest: Sprouts are ready to harvest when about one inch across. If left too long on the stem they may split. Sprouts mature from the bottom of the stem upwards. Remove the leaves along with the sprouts. These hardy plants withstand light frost, which we believe improves the flavor.

Cabbage 'Mercury'

Chinese Cabbage 'Two Seasons Hybrid'

Cabbage Mustard Family Easy ○

Days to Harvest: 60–70 Early*; 72–85 Midseason*; 100 Fall or Winter type*

Days to Germinate: 3 to 10

Temperature to Germinate: 68 to 86 degrees Fahrenheit

Growth Temperature: 60 to 70 degrees Fahrenheit

Height: 9 to 18 inches

Characteristics: Cabbage has always been one of the most widely grown vegetables in the home garden. A good way to involve and interest a child in a vegetable garden is to grow a "five-headed monster" cabbage. Trick a spring cabbage into producing five or six heads instead of one by picking a head of cabbage when it is the size of a softball, but leaving 5 or 6 of the outer leaves on the plant. Each of these leaves will produce another small head before fall.

As a gardener you have a choice of early, midseason, or late varieties. The early varieties mature the quickest and are usually grown as a spring crop. The rounded or pointed heads are small to medium in size. Recommended varieties are 'Earliana', 'Stonehead Hybrid', and 'Emerald Cross'.

Red cabbage varieties, with round, dark-purplish red heads, are grown as a spring or fall crop as they store well. Recommended varieties: 'Red Acre', 'Scarlet O'Hara'.

Midseason varieties, with medium to large heads, are excellent when grown as a spring or fall crop. Try Burpee's 'Copenhagen Market'. Savoy-type cabbages, with curly, crinkled leaves, grow like midseason varieties. We recommend 'Savoy Ace Hybrid'.

Slowest to mature are the late-winter or fall crops. They have large round or flat heads and keep well when properly stored. They are excellent for making sauerkraut. Recommended varieties: 'Burpee Surehead', 'Danish Roundhead'.

Cultural Information: When growing a spring crop, start early and midseason varieties indoors about six weeks before the last heavy spring frost. Water well. Cabbage tolerates a light spring frost. Supply plenty of water during prolonged dry spells. Cool, moist conditions are necessary for good growth. Cabbage are heavy feeders and like a monthly side dressing.

For a fall crop, start mid-season, Savoy, or the late varieties in mid- to late June in a cold frame or seedbed, and set the plants in the garden in early August.

Common pests include aphids, beetles, and cabbage worms. The most serious pests and diseases can be avoided by rotating crops: Don't plant where cole crops were grown the previous year. (See "Planting Guide for Cole Crops," page 49.)

Harvest: Cabbage is ready to harvest when the heads are well-filled and hard. Cut through the stem just below the head and remove the tough, protective outer leaves. Early cabbage should be used soon after harvest, preferably for salads or cole slaw.

Late varieties, grown for fall crops, are excellent keepers and good for cooking and sauerkraut. Store the fall harvest in a cool cellar, shed, or refrigerator, where the heads will keep for several weeks.

Cabbage, Chinese Mustard Family Easy ○

Days to Harvest: 43 to 85*

Days to Germinate: 3 to 7

Temperature to Germinate: 68 to 86 degrees Fahrenheit

Growth Temperature: 60 to 70 degrees

Height: 18 to 20 inches

Characteristics: Chinese cabbage has a sweet, mild flavor. It is normally grown as a fall crop; some varieties, like 'Two Seasons Hybrid', are reliable as both a spring and fall crop in most areas. The heads are either oval or tall and narrow, with thick, succulent ribs and crinkled, light-green leaves.

Cultural Information: Follow cultural information for cabbages. For spring crops, start indoors 8 to 10 weeks before the last heavy frost; seeds for a fall crop can be direct sown. The most common pests are aphids; the most common diseases are downy mildew and viral wilt. Chinese cabbage can be blanched for milder flavor by growing under a large milk carton (with two sides open) over the cabbage. (See "Planting Guide for Cole Crops," page 49.)
Harvest: Harvest as for Cabbage.

Carrots Parsley Family Easy ○

Days to Harvest: 60 to 90
Days to Germinate: 6 to 21
Temperature to Germinate: 68 to 86 degrees Fahrenheit
Growth Temperature: 60 to 80 degrees
Height: 3½ to 7½ inches
Characteristics: Carrots are delicious at all stages of their growth. Many sizes and shapes are available (see the carrot chart, above). Young carrot tops can be used for flavoring soup. I use the beautiful, feathery foliage in bouquets. (If some carrots are left unharvested over the winter, they will produce lovely flowers, similar to Queen Anne's Lace, before going to seed.) The tastiest carrots usually are those sown in early spring, but later sowings extend the harvest into fall and winter. If your soil is heavy clay, plant a shorter type, like 'Short n' Sweet'. In light soil, varieties like 'Imperator' or 'Toudo Hybrid' thrive.
Cultural Information: Carrots grow best in soil that has been deeply worked. As for all root vegetables, remove any stones to ensure proper, unimpeded root development. Good drainage is important to prevent rot and disease. Work compost into your soil to make it light and moisture-retentive. When grown in a raised bed with an extra depth of topsoil, the shape of carrots is much better. Wood ashes spread over the surface and raked into soil will provide a good source of potassium for sweeter-tasting carrots.

Best planted ¾ inch deep and 4 inches apart in moist soil that has warmed. After germination, thin until they stand about 3 inches apart and mulch to protect their roots from the hot sun.
Harvest: Harvest while still young for the peak of flavor, crunchiness, and nutrition. For winter use, carrots can be left in the garden until severe frost, then stored in a cool, humid spot with their tops removed.

Cantaloupe; see *Melons*

Cauliflower Mustard Family Moderately Challenging ○

Days to Harvest: 60*
Days to Germinate: 3 to 10
Temperature to Germinate: 68 to 86 degrees Fahrenheit
Growth Temperature: 60 to 70 degrees Fahrenheit
Height: 2½ feet
Characteristics: Cauliflower heads are made up of tightly packed white, mounded immature flower buds called "curds." When the heads reach 2 to 4 inches across, the curds should be "blanched" to produce the whitest, most attractive heads. To blanch, fold the outer leaves loosely over each head and secure them with a rubber band. Some varieties have leaves which tend to cover and protect the heads without tying.

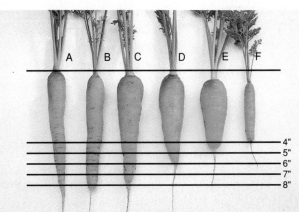

Choose the variety that's best for you
A. Imperator B. Toudo C. Royal Chantenay
D. Goldinhart E. Short n' Sweet F. Little Finger

'Purple Head' is one such variety, needing no blanching; it is easy to grow—though it takes a little longer—and is delicious, with a mild broccoli flavor.

Grow cauliflower as a spring or a fall crop. A minimum of eight weeks of cool weather is needed for proper development. In the spring, start the seeds indoors six to eight weeks before the last heavy frost. Cauliflower retains its flavor when refrigerated and freezes well. 'Early White Hybrid' is recommended by Burpee breeders as the best early cauliflower, with heads up to 9 inches across that don't become loose or ricey. The close jacket leaves encourage self-blanching.
Cultural Information: Same as Cabbage. Don't hold transplants too long after their roots have filled their container or they will "button" (form miniature heads). (See "Planting Guide for Cole Crops," page 49.) Varieties: 'Early Snowball', 'Snow Crown Hybrid', 'Early White Hybrid'.
Harvest: Harvest as soon as the heads are firm and reach the desired size. If left too long on the plant, the heads may become loose ("ricey") or discolored.

Cauliflower 'Candid Charm Hybrid'

Celery 'Tall Utah'

Collard 'Champion Hybrid'

Celery Parsley Family Moderately Challenging ○
Days to Harvest: 105 to 115*
Days to Germinate: 10 to 21
Temperature to Germinate: 50 to 86 degrees Fahrenheit
Growth Temperature: 60 to 70 degrees Fahrenheit
Height: 15 to 18 inches
Characteristics: Celery as we know it today is quite different from the strong-flavored celery grown and used as medicine around 1600. The mild, crisp stalks are usually eaten raw, and the leafy green tops are chopped and added to salads and soups. Braised celery makes a fine side dish. 'Tall Utah 52-70® Improved' has long, thick, dark green stalks and is resistant to boron deficiency and western celery mosaic.
Cultural Information: Celery requires a rich, moist soil and takes almost twice as long as most of the greens to mature. It requires a long growing season. Most gardeners start celery indoors three months before outdoor planting. It prefers a soil with a pH of 5.8 to 6.7. Before planting, work plenty of organic material into the soil to help hold moisture. Celery roots are shallow and demand constant moisture to grow. Lack of water slows growth and toughens the stalks, giving them a strong flavor. Like the majority of greens, celery needs cool weather to develop well, and is grown for spring or fall crops (in Zones 6 and higher it's best to grow celery as a fall crop). Sow the seeds indoors, ten weeks before the last heavy spring frost, or in late spring for a fall crop. Seeds are slow to germinate but can be speeded up by soaking in warm water overnight. Transplant the seedlings to the garden when they are about 5 inches tall. Before you set the plants, make a trench several inches deep. This will help shade and blanch the lower stems as well as collect water run-off for the thirsty roots. Then plant the crowns a little lower than the soil level, and water well. Cultivate or mulch to control weeds because celery cannot tolerate competition for water. Keep the plantings well-watered throughout the growing season. To blanch for white stalks and milder flavor, continue to add soil, compost or sand around the base of the stalks to just below the leaves; the plants will grow, reaching for the light.
Harvest: When large enough to eat, harvest the larger, outer stalks as you need them. The center will continue to produce stalks. To harvest big plants at the end of the season, pull up the whole plant and trim roots.

Collards Mustard Family Easy ○
Days to Harvest: 60
Days to Germinate: 3 to 10
Temperature to Germinate: 68 to 86 degrees Fahrenheit
Growth Temperature: 75 to 80 degrees Fahrenheit
Height: 2 to 3 feet
Characteristics: Rich in vitamins A and C, collards are traditionally a southern favorite. The leaves, blue-green and juicy, are delicious when boiled. The mild cabbage flavor is improved after a fall frost. These hardy plants can withstand lower temperatures than cabbage, growing in temperatures as low as 10 degrees Fahrenheit. Sow in spring for a summer crop, in midsummer for a fall crop. You can harvest the whole plant or just the young outer leaves, allowing the rest of the plant to continue to grow and produce more leaves for harvest. Delicious with ham or bacon. 'Georgia' is a popular variety that bears a loose cluster of slightly crumpled blue-green leaves. 'Vates' is lower growing with a compact habit and thicker, broader leaves. (See "Planting Guide for Leafy Greens," page 42.)
Cultural Information: Sow seeds directly in the garden in early spring. Collards like a loamy, well-drained soil with pH 6.8. Work in a slow-release 5–10–10 fertilizer before planting. Plant seeds ¼ inch deep, spaced 2 to 3 inches apart in rows 24 to 30 inches wide. Mature plants should stand 10 to 12 inches apart. One month after planting, apply fertilizer again or well-rotted manure. Mulch well after heavy frost in fall, as some plants will overwinter. Check frequently for aphids.
Harvest: Harvest only the bottom leaves of the plant as soon as there are enough for a meal. The center bud will keep putting out branches.

Corn, Sweet or Ornamental Grass Family Moderately Challenging ○
Days to Harvest: 60 to 85
Days to Germinate: 4 to 7
Temperature to Germinate: 68 to 86 degrees Fahrenheit
Growth Temperature: 80 degrees Fahrenheit
Height: 4½ to 9 feet
Characteristics: Everyone knows corn is a Native American vegetable, introduced to the early

settlers by Native American people. The Indian name, maize, means "bread of life." Sweet corn as we know it today didn't come into existence until the turn of this century. Breeders have introduced many new sweet varieties, with many colors: all-white, all-yellow, and yellow and white speckled for eating, 'Strawberry Ornamental Popcorn' for popping, and 'Rainbow' for decoration.

A good standard yellow variety is 'Early Sunglow', harvested in 63 days with each stalk yielding two ears, 7 inches long. A late white variety, worth waiting for, is 'Silver Queen', harvested in 92 days with large 8- to 9-inch ears. Newer varieties with the sugar enhancer gene, SE gene, significantly raises kernel sugar content above standard hybrids while retaining the tenderness and creamy texture. Higher initial sugar content allows them to stay sweet and tender for 10 to 14 days after reaching maturity. 'Breeder's Choice' is the earliest of the sugar enhancer types, and our research director's favorite among all sweet corn varieties in our trials, hence the name. Burpee's 'Peppy Hybrid', harvested in 90 days, is an outstanding, high-yield variety grown for popping. *Cultural Information:* Direct sow corn outdoors when soil temperature has reached 60 degrees Fahrenheit. The soil should have lots of organic matter, best incorporated in fall to allow time for it to decompose. Before planting, work in a slow-release 5–10–10 fertilizer along the planting rows; corn is a heavy feeder.

It is best to block plant corn, in at least three or four short rows next to each other, to help the wind pollinate the flowers. If corn is planted in fewer rows, chances are that most of the pollen will just blow away rather than onto a nearby corn plant. Plant seed 2 inches deep and approximately 6 inches apart. Mature plants should stand 16 inches apart. Your crop will need lots of water to produce a healthy ear of corn. Mulch to control weeds and help retain moisture.

The most common diseases are bacterial wilt and leaf blights. Other problems are 1) Lack of ears: If your planting doesn't produce well, it could be due to crowding of the plants, insufficient sunlight, or a too-high nitrogen content in the soil. 2) Poorly filled ears: This is due to poor or incomplete pollination. Sometimes weather conditions can interfere with pollen transfer from tassel to silk, but most often this problem is due to planting in long, single rows. 3) Stunted plants with yellow lower leaves: This indicates nitrogen deficiency. Fertilizer or fish emulsion should help. If plants are stunted and leaves show reddish streaks, this may indicate phosphorus deficiency. 4) Leaf Roll: Leaves of some varieties roll up during the day, then unroll at night. In the case of other varieties, however, this can be the first sign the plants need water.

Harvest: The sooner after harvesting sweet corn is eaten, the better. Once corn is picked, the sugar starts to turn to starch. Some newer varieties such as 'Breeders Choice' have been bred to keep longer without turn-

ing starchy. Corn is ready to harvest when the silks turn brown and the ears fill the husks. When you pierce a kernel with your fingernail, the liquid inside should be milky. If it is watery, it is too early to pick; when it is creamy, it is too late.

Crowder pea; see *Beans, Cowpea*

Top: Sweet corn 'Silver Queen'
Above: Ornamental corn 'Carousel'

Top: Cucumber 'Bush Champion'
Above: Cucumber 'Armenian'

Cucumbers Gourd Family

Easy ○

Days to Harvest: 50 to 70
Days to Germinate: 3 to 7
Temperature to Germinate: 68 to 86 degrees Fahrenheit
Growth Temperature: 60 to 70 degrees Fahrenheit
Height: 4½ to 9 feet
Characteristics: Cucumbers, more than 90 percent water, were used in ancient times to quench thirst on desert trips. Today they are a favorite for salads and pickling. Cucumbers are easy to grow and come in handy small-space varieties and drought- and disease-resistant hybrids. Most cucumbers are green with a bumpy skin, but there are smooth-skinned varieties too. Slicing cucumbers grow to a length of 8 to 10 inches and are available in standard and hybrid varieties. "Burpless" types produce fruit with tender skin and fewer seeds, making them easily digestible. This latter type is perfect for pickles and salads; try them sliced and mixed with sour cream.

Armenian and lemon types are fun to grow, adding a conversation piece and gourmet touch to your garden. The Armenian cucumbers, light-green and heavily ribbed, can grow to 3 feet or more, staying deliciously sweet and mild with few seeds. Their thin skin has no bitterness and needs no peeling. Lemon cucumbers look like lemons, but don't have a lemon flavor. Very sweet (they never become bitter with age), they are for the gardener who likes to try something new; because they are filled with seeds, use them young before the seeds are large and tough.

All cucumbers make good pickles, but the smaller types, 2 to 4 inches, are preferred and are hard to find in stores. 'Burpee Pickler' is an all-purpose cucumber especially good for pickling. (When you grow cucumbers for pickling, plant dill in your garden too. Then you're set with the fresh ingredients you'll need at pickling time.)

If you're anxious for high yields, choose the special hybrid group of gynoecious cucumbers. Gynoecious cucumbers bear only female flowers and produce very heavily. When you buy these varieties, you'll find a few seeds of a pollinator are included to ensure good fruit set. Several varieties like 'Early Pride Hybrid' and 'Burpee Hybrid II' are available for the home garden, with pollinator-type seeds for good fruit set. If your garden space is limited, grow bush-type varieties as they take only one-third the space the usual vining types do. Bush types are ideal in large containers, too.

Cultural Information: Cucumbers like long, hot days and warm nights. Sow seeds after the danger of frost is past to ensure a successful planting. Plant in fertile soil that has good drainage. Plant seeds 1 inch deep, approximately 6 inches apart. Mature plants should stand 1 to 2 feet apart. If you are planting in hills (see page 79), plant four seeds about 6 feet apart and thin to the best seedlings. Soil must be kept moist. One month after planting, apply a second application of fertilizer or compost around the base of plants. This is also a good time to add mulch.

The most common pests are aphids, cucumber beetles, squash bugs, and vine borers. The most common diseases are anthracnose, powdery mildew, and bacterial wilt.

If you train cucumbers to grow up on a trellis or stakes, the fruit set will increase. Staking cucumbers reduces the incidence of fruit rot because the fruit is less crowded and has better air circulation. Trained plants need more water unless the soil is well-mulched. (See "Planting Guide for Vine Crops," page 55.)

Harvest: Like all vine crops, cucumbers will be more productive if they are picked often, and they may be picked at different stages of growth up to maturity, depending on how they are to be used. Most are at their best when yellow, not green, and the flesh firm and crisp. However, at this stage the seeds are tough and have to be removed. You can harvest different sizes of cucumbers at

PLANTING GUIDE FOR VINE CROPS

VARIETY	WHEN TO SOW	SEED PLANTING DEPTH	SPACING* HILL CULTURE†	ROW CULTURE	DAYS TO GERMINATE	DAYS TO HARVEST
CUCUMBERS, Vining types	After all danger of frost; second sowing 4–5 weeks later.	½"	Plant 5–6 seeds, each 2–3" apart, in hills 4–6' apart. Thin to 2–3 plants per hill.	Plant seeds 4–6" apart in rows 3' apart. Thin plants to 12" apart.	7–14	50–70
Bush types	Same as above.	½"		Plant seeds 4–6" apart in rows 3' apart. Thin plants to 12" apart.	7–14	50–70
GOURDS	After all danger of frost.	1"	Plant 4–5 seeds, each 2–3" apart, in hills 6' apart. Thin to 3–4 plants per hill.		7–14	100–120
MELONS, Cantaloupes, Casaba, Crenshaw & Honey Dew Melons	After all danger of frost.	½"	Plant 4–8 seeds, each 2–3" apart, in hills 4–6' apart. Thin to 2–3 plants per hill.	Plant seeds 6" apart in rows 5–6' apart. Thin to 12" apart.	7–14	75–120
PUMPKINS, Vining types	After all danger of frost.	1"	Plant 5–6 seeds, each 2–3" apart, in hills 6–8' apart. Thin to 2 plants per hill.		7–14	100–120
Bush types	Same as above.	1"		Plant seeds 1–2' apart in rows 6' apart. Thin plants to 3' apart.	7–14	95
SQUASH, Summer	After all danger of frost; second sowing 8 weeks before first expected fall frost.	1"	Plant 4–6 seeds, each 2–3" apart, in hills 3–4' apart. Thin to 2–3 plants per hill.	Plant seeds 6" apart in rows 3–4' apart. Thin plants to 18" apart.	10–14	50–60
SQUASH, Winter Vining types	After all danger of frost.	1"	Plant 6 or more seeds, each 2–3" apart, in hills 6–8' apart. Thin to 3–4 plants per hill.		7–14	80–120

*Spacing information is approximate. Vine crops are so diverse in growth habit (length of vines) that even similar varieties will sometimes differ in spacing recommendations. Therefore, *please read all packet instructions* before planting.
†Planting in "hills" is a term used to denote the method of planting seeds in clusters. These groups need not be planted in raised mounds to form "hills."

VEGETABLES

PLANTING GUIDE FOR VINE CROPS

VARIETY	WHEN TO SOW	SEED PLANTING DEPTH	SPACING* HILL CULTURE†	ROW CULTURE	DAYS TO GERMINATE	DAYS TO HARVEST
Bush types	Same as vining types, page 55.	1″	Plant 3–4 seeds, each 2–3″ apart, in hills 3′ apart. Thin to 1–2 plants per hill.		7–14	75–80
WATER-MELONS, Vining types	After all danger of frost.	½″	Plant 5–6 seeds, each 2–3″ apart, in hills 6–8′ apart. Thin to 2–3 plants per hill.	Plant seeds 12″ apart in rows 6–7′ apart. Thin plants to 2–3″ ft. apart.	10	70–90
Bush types	Same as above.	½″	Plant 5–6 seeds, each 2–3″ apart, in hills 3–3½′ apart. Thin to 2–3 plants per hill.	Plant seeds 12″ apart in rows 3–3½′ apart. Thin plants to 2′ apart.	10	70–90

*Spacing information is approximate. Vine crops are so diverse in growth habit (length of vines) that even similar varieties will sometimes differ in spacing recommendations. Therefore, *please read all packet instructions* before planting.
†Planting in "hills" is a term used to denote the method of planting seeds in clusters. These groups need not be planted in raised mounds to form "hills."

the same time, small ones for sweet pickles, larger ones for bread and butter pickles, dill pickles, or for slicing. For the best flavor, harvest full-size cucumbers before the seeds become well developed. Pickling cucumbers normally will be 2 to 6 inches long. Cucumbers for slicing should be 6 to 10 inches long. The "burpless" type

needs to be harvested when under 10 inches long and about 1½ inches in diameter. Armenian cucumbers should be picked before they exceed 2½ inches in diameter.

Curlicress; see ***Garden cress***

Eggplant Nightshade Family Easy ○
Days to Harvest: 55 to 70*
Days to Germinate: 7 to 14
Temperature to Germinate: 70 to 75 degrees Fahrenheit
Growth Temperature: 75 to 80 degrees Fahrenheit
Height: 2 to 3 feet
Characteristics: Eggplant is beautiful from flower to fruit with its purple, star-shaped flowers over an inch across and glossy, deep purple fruits. Eggplant bears its shiny, pendant fruits close to the main stem. The fruits

are essential in many splendid dishes: French ratatouille, Italian caponata, and Greek moussaka, among others. They're delicious sliced and simply fried. Most varieties have broad, blunt, oval fruit, but some oriental types bear long and slender fruits. The skin is usually purple, but white, yellow, and green varieties exist. Whatever the color, the flavor is much the same. 'Millionaire' is an exceptionally handsome Japanese type, long and thin. 'Black Beauty', an old favorite, is tender and tasty at all stages. 'Burpee Hybrid' is a tall plant, semi-spreading and very vigorous. 'Early Beauty Hybrid' is one of the earliest, yet longest, producers.
Cultural Information: Eggplant likes a warm, fertile soil that is well-drained. This is one of the most heat- and drought-

Eggplant 'Dusky Hybrid'

56

tolerant vegetables. Wait about two weeks after you plant out your tomatoes before placing eggplant in the garden. Eggplant is very cold-sensitive; blossoms start to drop if temperatures drop below 50°. Cover with a garden blanket or floating row cover to keep them cozy at night. It needs a warm soil for healthy growth. A raised bed heats up faster and is ideal. Sow seeds indoors 8 to 10 weeks before transplanting to the garden, 1 to 2 weeks after the last frost. When transplanting into the garden, allow 2 feet between plants, and 3 feet between rows. When plants are 6 inches tall, pinch off growing tips to encourage branching. Eggplant appreciate a feeding of fish emulsion or fertilizer every 3 or 4 weeks.

Black plastic can be used to warm the soil before planting, and to hold the heat and moisture after planting. A healthy handful of well-rotted manure should be worked into the planting hole. About a month after planting apply a second application of fertilizer. Use a mulch to control weeds and cover with plastic. A common problem is the potato beetle, and infestations can cause the disease verticillium wilt. There is no cure for this disease, which can live in the soil for years and devastate plants. Avoid growing eggplant in soil where peppers, tomatoes, or potatoes recently—in the last two seasons—grew. If verticillium wilt persists, grow in 5-gallon containers (with drainage holes) filled with disease-free soil, giving the plants a southern exposure. Water daily and feed weekly.

Harvest: Eggplant can be picked at any size; look for firm, glossy fruits. Harvest while the skin is shiny. When overmature, fruits become dull-skinned, brownish, bitter, and filled with seeds. To harvest, hold fruit firmly at the blossom end and cut off with a pruning shears or knife just above the calyx (cap), leaving a little of the stem attached. Eggplant is prickly at the stem and calyx, so handle carefully. Most plants produce 4 to 6 eggplants, but if you keep picking, the plants continue to produce. Cook as soon as possible after harvesting. Fruits taste best cooked fresh or cooked and frozen.

Endive, Chicory, Escarole Sunflower Family Easy ○

Days to Harvest: 65 to 110
Days to Germinate: 5 to 14
Temperature to Germinate: 68 to 80 degrees Fahrenheit
Growth Temperature: 60 to 70 degrees
Height: 16 to 18 inches
Characteristics: These slightly pungent, tasty salad greens are gorgeous in the garden, window box, or other container. Endive is an attractive frilly, green form, while escarole is more broad-leafed and slightly crumpled. Chicory (French or Belgian endive) with its smooth, sleek leaves is a gourmet treat with a tantalizing, bitter flavor. Radicchio is a red form of chicory with a sharp flavor all its own; it is sometimes grilled. All are tasty and inviting in salads and all can be grown for spring or fall crops. Although naturally bitter plants, especially if grown in hot weather, they are most desirable with just a touch of bitterness. Because hot weather can make the leaves extremely

Top: Chicory 'Sugar Hat'
Above: Chicory 'Radicchio, Marina'

bitter, many gardeners blanch the hearts by tying the outer leaves over the center of the plants about two or three weeks before the harvest. This makes the hearts turn pale gold or creamy white, and improves the texture and flavor of the leaves. The plants stand light frost well and have better flavor if grown as a fall crop.

Green curled endive with its rich green, finely cut fringed leaves is ready to harvest in 90 days. Chicory, 'Witloof' is recommended for outdoor planting or indoor forcing and can be harvested in 110 days. Radicchio, 'Marina' is ready in 110 days with 8- to 12-ounce, dark red heads.

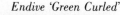

Endive 'Green Curled'

Cultural Information: These greens are grown under the same culture as lettuce, though they are less heat-sensitive than lettuce. They are seldom bothered by disease. Endive is long-lasting in the garden.

Chicory, 'Witloof' (French or Belgian endive) can be forced indoors in the winter; the roots, shaped like carrots, produce creamy yellow, blanched "chicons," prized by gourmets for salads and braising. For continued harvest over the winter, harvest and cut the root to 6 to 8 inches long. Place roots close together, ends down, in a 12- to 16-inch-deep box. Fill the box with peat moss and sand, covering the roots to a depth of 6 to 8 inches to exclude light. Water thoroughly and cover the box with a mat or board to keep out the light and keep in the moisture. Store in a cool, dark place at 60 degrees Fahrenheit. In four to five weeks the tips of the heads will break through the surface. Cut when they are 5 to 6 inches long by reaching down through the soil and cutting just above the root with a sharp knife.

Harvest: Harvest chicory, endive, and escarolelike lettuce; heads store well.

Opposite, from top:
Garden cress;
Garden rocket;
Garlic

Fennel 'Zefa Fino'

Fennel Parsley Family Easy ○

Days to Harvest: 80
Days to Germinate: 10 to 21
Temperature to Germinate: 70 degrees Fahrenheit
Growth Temperature: 65 degrees Fahrenheit
Height: 2½ feet
Characteristics: Fennel, sometimes called "anise," has a flavor somewhat like that of licorice. The plant grows to about 2 feet tall with broad stalks and fern-like leaves. Discard tough outer leaves. Slice stalks and serve with oil and spices. Young leaves and stems are used in salads, and vegetable and egg dishes. Fennel bulbs are cooked as vegetables. The dried seeds flavor desserts, pickles, baked goods, and candy. 'Florence' is a popular green-leaved variety; 'Bronze' has handsome, bronze-colored leaves.
Cultural Information: Fennel requires cool weather and can be direct sown in a sunny spot as soon as soil can be worked. A second crop can be planted in late summer. Sow seed ¼ inch deep. Mature plants should stand 18 inches apart. Fennel needs to be blanched, so build up soil around the bottom halfway through the growing season; this will ensure a paler, more tender vegetable. Fennel is relatively pest-free (the fragrance seems to repel insects), but slugs can be a problem if you use mulch and water often.
Harvest: Cut the plant just below the soil when it reaches 2 to 3 inches in diameter. New growth will appear from the base left in the ground. You can also harvest a stalk at a time as you need it. Remove the leaves and use fresh or dried as you would fennel. Store fennel bulbs in ice water in the refrigerator for a day or so. Or, separate the stalks from the base and store in a plastic bag in the refrigerator for several days. Seeds can be harvested (if the plant is allowed to go to seed).

Garbanzo beans; see Beans, Chick peas

Garden Cress (Curlicress) Easy ○◑

Days to Harvest: 10 to 14
Days to Germinate: 4 to 10
Temperature to Germinate: 68 degrees Fahrenheit
Growth Temperature: 70 to 80 degrees Fahrenheit
Height: a few inches
Characteristics: Easy and quick to grow, Garden cress has tiny, finely curled leaves with a pungent flavor. They are delicious in salads, dips, spreads, or for garnish. Sprouted seeds are tasty in salads and sandwiches. The plants make a pretty border for a flower or vegetable garden.
Cultural Information: In a pot in a sunny windowsill, Garden cress can be grown year-round, harvested as few as 10 days after sowing. It can be sown outdoors, from early spring to fall, in a partly shaded area to avoid afternoon sun. Garden cress can be grown outdoors all year round in the Deep South, Gulf Coast, and Pacific Coast areas. It prefers fertile, moist soil. Crops are very short-lived, so sow every two weeks for a constant supply. Because it is harvested so quickly, thinning Garden cress is unnecessary. This plant is relatively pest-free. (See "Planting Guide for Leafy Greens" page 42.)

Harvest: Harvest when very young, using scissors to cut off at the soil line.

Garden Rocket (Roquette, Argula, Rugula) Mustard Family Easy ○

Days to Harvest: 35
Days to Germinate: 7 to 14
Temperature to Germinate: 60 to 70 degrees Fahrenheit
Growth Temperature: 60 to 70 degrees Fahrenheit
Height: under 6 inches are tastiest, but will grow to 2 feet tall
Characteristics: Rocket, related to mustard, was introduced to America by 17th century settlers and has been grown here ever since. This European favorite matures quickly, producing deeply cut leaves that are pungent, robust, and peppery when young. The foliage looks like a cross between the leaves of radish and dandelion. Use the young leaves in salads, mature leaves mixed with other greens. Grow for a spring or fall crop. The flowers also are edible and are nice in salads and as garnishes.
Cultural Information: Grow during the cooler part of the season. Plants grown in hot weather are bitter. The plants grow best in well-drained soil and need plenty of moisture. Resow every two or three weeks for a steady supply. Pull up plants after flowering and before they go to seed. Arugula, like many leafy crops, are relatively free of pests and diseases, but flea beetles may be a problem. Garden blankets will keep them off. Plant repellent plants such as garlic or catnip nearby (in the next row—up to 3 feet away it will still be effective).

Harvest: Harvest pale green leaves no larger than 6 inches. Cut at soil line and leave the roots for continuous growth. To store, pull up with roots, wrap in damp cloth or paper toweling, and refrigerate in a plastic bag up to three or four days.

Garlic Allium Family Easy ○

Days to Harvest: 100
Growth Temperature: 70 to 80 degrees Fahrenheit
Height: 12 to 24 inches
Characteristics: This is an ancient vegetable; there are even references to it in the Old Testament. In addition to its importance as a flavoring, garlic is a delicious food in itself. Try roasting entire bulb clusters until soft; the delicious, mild flavor will amaze and delight you. Garlic is reported to have beneficial effects on blood pressure. The flowers are handsome in arrangements. For a milder garlic, try Elephant garlic. The flavor of these huge bulbs, each with several enormous cloves, adds a gentle zing. Elephant garlic is available from Burpee in the fall only, starting in September, as we have found fall planting preferable for best production. Winter protection is needed in the North.
Cultural Information: Choose a well-drained spot in full sun. Garlic bulbs are made up of numerous sections ("cloves," divided by papery membrane.) Separate the cloves before planting. Plant cloves 3 inches deep and approximately 3 inches apart in mid-spring. In the North, plant in early spring or fall; in the South and Pacific Southwest, plant in fall. Grow, harvest, and store like onions. With

no known pests or disease, garlic is itself often used as an all-around insect and disease deterrent.

Harvest: Garlic is ready to harvest when tops turn brown and fall over. When many of the tops have turned yellow and fallen over, crimp the remaining tops to hasten ripening. Harvest bulbs and store at 40 to 60 degrees Fahrenheit.

Globe artichoke; see *Artichoke*

Gourds Gourd Family Easy ○

Days to Harvest: 90–100
Days to Germinate: 7–14
Temperature to Germinate: 68 to 86 degrees Fahrenheit
Growth Temperature: 70 to 85 degrees Fahrenheit
Characteristics: Gourds are used primarily for decoration, although some are edible. There are three types of gourd, but the majority of those grown by home gardeners are *Cucurbita*.

Cucurbita gourds can be kept as ornaments only three to four months, unlike the *Lagenaria* gourds, which will last for years if properly treated. *Lagenaria* gourds have thinner shells and a longer growing season than the *Cucurbita*. These white-flowered gourds have the unusual shapes that make them suitable for craft projects (they have been used to make rattles, dippers, and birdhouses, among other things.) If you prefer straight necks, grow them on fences or trellises, to prevent their necks from curling. 'Turk's Turban' is a particular favorite because of its brilliant orange and yellow color and its interesting (turbanlike) shape.

Some of the more popular varieties of *Lagenaria* are the 'Large Bottle', 'Calabash', 'Dolphin', 'Dipper', 'Hercules Club', and 'Swan' gourds.

The last of the three gourd types is *Luffa*, known also as vegetable sponge, sponge gourd, or dishrag gourd. Many people use the fibrous material inside the unusual gourd as a sponge after the gourd has grown to maturity. Like the other gourds, *Luffa* can easily be trained to a trellis or fence.

Gourds can be shaped with tape or string while young to assume any shape you wish. You can even grow them inside plastic jars to mould their shapes; when the gourd has filled the jar, carefully cut off the plastic. Gourds continue to grow, holding the shape into which they were initially trained. Children can scratch initials or designs into the skin of the fruit, and watch the designs grow as the fruit grows.

Cultural Information: Gourds are grown like winter squash. Seeds can be started in peat pots in cooler climates three to four weeks before planting outside in the garden. Mature plants should stand 2 feet apart. Their soil requirements and pest and disease problems are the same as those of winter squash and cucumbers. Plastic mulch is recommended. (See "Planting Guide for Vine Crops," page 55.)
Harvest: Gourds should be harvested before the first frost of fall, leaving 1 to 2 inches of stem on the fruit. They must then be cured for several days in a shaded spot under warm, dry conditions. When cured, seeds will make a rattling sound

when the gourd is shaken. Some varieties of *Lagenaria* gourds take up to six months to cure. Once cured, a gourd can be cut, carved, hollowed out, lacquered, varnished, painted, or waxed.

'Dipper' and 'Birdhouse' gourds are easily made into low-cost wren houses. Harvest a suitable gourd, remove the thin outer skin with a knife and then dry the fruit in a warm, shaded place. When the gourd is dry, bore or cut a smooth, round hole the size of a quarter in the side of the large part of the gourd, then drill a smaller hole completely through the stem end. The small hole is for the hanging wire. Use a spoon handle or a dull knife to loosen the dried seeds and fibers so that they can be shaken out through the large hole. Finally, paint the surface with shellac or polyurethane, if you want to preserve the gourd for more than one season.

After harvesting and curing *Luffa* gourds, peel the skin off under running water as you would peel an orange. Let dry, then shake the seeds out from the inner sponge.

Haricots verts; see *Beans*

Kale Mustard Family Easy ○
Days to Harvest: 50–65
Days to Germinate: 3 to 10
Temperature to Germinate: 68 to 86 degrees Fahrenheit
Growth Temperature: 60 to 70 degrees Fahrenheit
Height: 12 to 16 inches
Characteristics: Kale is an attractive addition to the fall garden. It has a green to blue-green leaf with fringed or curly edges. Blanch and stuff the leaves, or

Gourds 'Small Fancy'

Kale 'Dwarf Blue Curled Vates'

cook with collards and other greens. (See "Planting Guide for Leafy Greens," page 42.)

Cultural Information: Kale prefers cool weather, and frost improves the flavor. Seeds can be directly planted in the garden in early spring. Keep the soil moist for good germination. A second crop can be planted in late summer. Mature plants should stand 2 feet apart.

The plants form large rosettes of beautiful, curled leaves with high vitamin content and flavor similar to that of cabbage. Sow seed in average soil in early spring for a summer crop, late summer for a fall crop. In the Deep South, Gulf Coast, or Pacific Coast areas, sow the seeds in fall for an early spring crop. Cultivate the soil frequently to keep it loose and weed-free. Check for aphids and spray as needed.

Harvest: The leaves may be harvested at any time but are better before they are fully developed. The leaves are delicious raw, but can be cooked and used like spinach.

Kohlrabi Mustard Family Easy ○

Days to Harvest: 40 to 60
Days to Germinate: 3 to 10
Temperature to Germinate: 68 to 86 degrees Fahrenheit
Growth Temperature: 60 to 70 degrees Fahrenheit
Height: 6 to 8 inches
Characteristics: If ever a vegetable looked like it dropped to planet Earth from outer space, this is it. Kohlrabi grow from erect stems to form a turniplike bulb just above ground. Curving stems grow out of the side as well as the top of the edible bulb; the bulb forms on the soil surface instead of underground, which looks very peculiar. The greenish-white flesh with green or purple skin adds to the strange appearance. Widely used in Europe, kohlrabi deserves more attention in the United States. When young, about 2 to 2½ inches across, the flesh has a very mild, sweet, turniplike flavor. Though kohlrabi is a relative of cabbage, the flavor is sweeter than that of cabbage or turnip. Delicious raw, or steamed or boiled and served with a cream sauce. 'Grand Duke Hybrid' is extra early, 45 to 50 days, with round bulbs of crisp white flesh; 'Early Purple Vienna', 60 days, has round purplish bulbs with greenish white flesh. Pests rarely bother it.

Cultural Information: Like cabbage, Kohlrabi likes a cool growing season. Rich, loamy soil, with pH 6.0 to 7.5, is ideal. Direct sow in early spring and harvest long before the heat of summer. Sow again in midsummer for a fall crop. Thin plants to 3 to 4 inches apart.

Harvest: Kohlrabi has the best flavor when 2½ to 3 inches in diameter. Common pests are aphids and cabbage looper.

Leek Amaryllis Family Easy ○

Days to Harvest: 110 to 130 days
Days to Germinate: 6 to 14
Temperature to Germinate: 65 to 70 degrees Fahrenheit
Growth Temperature: 60 to 75 degrees Fahrenheit
Height: 8 inches
Characteristics: Leeks have a sweet, delicate flavor that makes them a favorite with gourmet cooks. They make superb soups and are delightful braised or cooked, then served cold with a vinaigrette. The stalks are white with blue-green leaves. Their foliage is attractive and they can be mixed in a flower border to be harvested after frost. 'Broad London', a 130-day variety with thick stems and mild flavor, is the best variety for over-wintering. 'Titan', a 110-day variety, has longer stalks, shanks up to 8 inches long and 1¾ to 2 inches across, with slightly bulbous bases; it is a popular earlier variety.

Cultural Information: Leeks can be started indoors eight to ten weeks before planting outdoors (after all danger of frost). They are ready to transplant to the garden when they are half the thickness of a pencil. They prefer deeply prepared, rich, loose, sandy loam. Plant in 4- to 6-inch-wide furrows which will hold the rain water and help to keep them moist. Mulch to keep weeds down and hold moisture. As they grow, gradually hill up around them with soil to just below the crown where the leaves start. This will keep the lower stem white and force the plant to stretch for the light, which will increase the length of the lower stem—the tender white part.

Harvest: Leeks are mature when the stems are 1 to 2 inches

Kohlrabi 'Grand Duke Hybrid'

Leek 'Titan'

thick and 6 to 8 inches long from roots to crown. Leave them in the ground and dig them up as you need them. They can stay all winter but must be heavily mulched with 18 or more inches of straw if you would like to be able to harvest them when the ground is frozen. They can be stored in moist sand, sawdust, or peat and put in a cool place with a constant temperature between 32 to 40 degrees Fahrenheit for two to three months. Before cooking, soak in cool water and wash thoroughly; soil stays trapped between the leaves and rings.

Below: Loosehead lettuce 'Ruby' and 'Black-Seeded Simpson'

Above: Loosehead lettuce 'Royal Oak Leaf
Right: Cos lettuce 'Paris White Cos'

Lettuce Sunflower Family
Shade on Hot Days Easy ○ ◐
Days to Harvest: 45 to 90
Days to Germinate: 7
Temperature to Germinate: 68 degrees Fahrenheit
Growth Temperature: 70 to 75 degrees Fahrenheit
Height: 9 to 15 inches
Characteristics: The varied colors and forms of lettuces make them beautiful in the garden. Fortunately for the new gardener they are very easy to grow. In fact, once planted, leafy greens are relatively trouble-free and reward the gardener with a tender, varied, always-delicious

harvest. Most greens like cool weather but some grow well into summer, so a little planning and proper choice of variety will bring you salads from early spring well past the first frost of winter.
General Cultural Information: All of the leafy greens can be direct sown in the garden. They have excellent yields when planted in early spring and later summer, and they are also good when planted in a semishady area in the summer (but for this, choose loosehead and butterhead types, and keep the soil moist).

Some problems for lettuce and other leafy greens are: 1) Tipburn, browning of the edges of the leaves, which may become serious during hot weather. Keep plants growing vigorously and keep soil evenly moist. Mulching will help. 2) Bitter taste is sometimes a problem when weather is hot during harvest. Store harvested leaves in the refrigerator for several days; bitterness will usually lessen. Exposure to freezing temperatures or soil nutrient deficiency can also cause bitterness. 3) Bolting (plants going to seed prematurely) occurs when weather is hot while plants are maturing. Plant early enough so crops develop before hot weather sets in; space plants properly for best light and air circulation. (See "Planting Guide for Leafy Greens," page 42.)
Harvest: Cut the head off at soil line, leaving roots in the ground where they will produce another crop.

HEAD LETTUCE

Butterhead

These plants produce small heads of tender, loosely folded leaves with a buttery texture. The outer leaves are green, the center leaves lightly golden. In hot regions, they may not head as well as crisp-head types but will grow rapidly and produce tender, tasty leaves. 'Burpee Bibb' is far superior to regular Bibb. Crisp texture, delicate flavor, no bitterness even in the outer leaves. It is slow-bolting with less tip-burn than most butterheads. For cultural information, see Lettuce.

Cos (Romaine)

Romaine has more of the daily vitamins we need than other leafy greens and is a good source of calcium. The upright plants form lightly folded, narrow heads, green on the outside and paler on the inside. 'Little Gem' is an English favorite with bright green leaves only 6 inches long. 'Parris Island Cos' has 8- to 10-inch heads of medium green, thick, slightly savoyed leaves and is slow to bolt.
Cultural Information: Plant these seeds a little more thickly than other varieties as Romaine doesn't germinate as well. Romaine takes a little longer to form a full head than the other varieties, about 70 to 80 days.

Crisphead (Iceberg)

This is still the most common lettuce at the grocery store. Because it requires a longer growing season, it's best to start seeds early indoors if you live in a northern climate. It produces young, firm heads of smooth, finely veined leaves with brittle texture. The outer leaves are medium green; inner leaves are pale green. 'Great Lakes' produces large, glistening, well-folded heads with fine flavor and crisp texture. For cultural information, see Lettuce.

LOOSELEAF

This is the easiest for home gardeners to grow. These mild-flavored, fast-maturing plants form thick branches of leaves which may be frilled or crumpled. Leaf color ranges from light green to deep red. Many varieties are heat-resistant, which means they are slow to go to seed and, consequently, edible for a longer time. 'Green Ice' is the least bitter of all lettuce in the Burpee trials. We highly recommend it. It has wonderful crisp texture, fine flavor and dark green, heavily crinkled leaves. 'Royal Oak Leaf' is a heat-tolerant, oak-leaflike, dark green leaf that produces well into hot summer weather. 'Ruby' will add interest and color to your salads with its bright green, frilled leaves, prominently shaded with intense red.

Cultural Information: All types grow best in cool weather. Plant as early as the ground can be worked, and plant successively about every two weeks in spring to extend the harvest. They will grow in midsummer if sown in a cool, semishady area. To delay bolting (premature flowering of a plant to make seed), pick continuously. It is best to plant again in late summer for a fall crop. Grows all winter in Zones 9 and 10. Sow seeds thinly ¼ to ½ inch apart. Thin seedlings to 4 to 12 inches apart, using thinnings for early salads.

Harvest: Leaf lettuce can be harvested by cutting off at the soil line, leaving the roots in the ground to cut another crop.

Melons Gourd Family Moderately Difficult ○

Days to Harvest: 75 to 120
Days to Germinate: 4 to 10
Temperature to Germinate: 68 to 86 degrees Fahrenheit
Growth Temperature: 65 to 60 degrees Fahrenheit
Characteristics: Cantaloupes (also called muskmelons) can be grown in nearly every part of the United States, since there are varieties suited to many soil, rain, and temperature conditions. With their firm, bright salmon flesh, they are sweet, juicy, and full of flavor. There are also early-maturing varieties such as Burpee's 'Sweet 'n Early Hybrid', ideal for short-season areas. 'Burpee Hybrid' and 'Ambrosia Hybrid' both have outstanding flavor.

Other melons—honeydew, casaba, and crenshaw—are "winter" melons because they ripen late in the season and can be kept a month or longer after being picked, provided they are stored in a cool, dry place. Honeydew melons have smooth, white or greenish-white skin and green flesh. Delicious early crop varieties are available; one is Burpee's 'Venus Hybrid', which ripens three weeks earlier than the standard variety.

Casaba melons, globe-shaped and pointed at the stem, ripen with a golden yellow skin and white flesh. Crenshaw melons are oval, their skin yellowish-tan and lightly netted. Inside is salmon-colored flesh with a delicious taste. Both varieties require a long season and do best in the Southwest. Crenshaws can grow large, up to 14 pounds.

Cultural Information: Melons should be grown like all vine crops. They are susceptible to frost and require warm temperatures for good growth. Wait for the soil to warm before planting seeds or setting out seedlings. Where the growing season is short, choose varieties that mature early and start the plants indoors three to four weeks before the anticipated outdoor planting. Plastic mulch is recommended to keep the soil warm and to keep the fruits off the ground. (It also eliminates weeding.) Where garden space is limited, cantaloupe vines can be trained up a fence or trellis and the fruit can be supported in cheesecloth or mesh slings. (Never use sprays or dusts containing sulfur on cantaloupe plants; they can burn the plants.)

Melons have the same pest and disease problems as cucumbers (See "Planting Guide for Vine Crops," page 55.)

Harvest: Most cantaloupes should be harvested when the fruit changes from green to yellow or tan and the netting of the skin becomes very pronounced. At the vine-ripe stage, the stem will slip cleanly away from the

Honeydew 'Venus Hybrid'

Cantaloupe 'Honeybush Hybrid'

fruit with only slight pressure.

Casaba, crenshaw, and most honeydew melons differ in that their stems do not slip away from the fruit when it is ripe. (An exception is 'Venus Hybrid' Honeydew.) These melons should be harvested when their fruits turn yellow and the blossom end (look for the blossom scar) gives to gentle pressure. Melons should be harvested only when the foliage is dry. Each vine normally produces three or four melons.

After you've eaten the melons, toss the rinds into the compost heap. Your plants will love the nutrients when you distribute the compost.

Mustard Greens Mustard Family Easy ○

Days to Harvest: 40 to 50
Temperature to Germinate: 68 to 86 degrees Fahrenheit
Days to Germinate: 3 to 7
Growth Temperature: 60 to 65 degrees Fahrenheit
Height: 15 to 18 inches
Characteristics: The plants tolerate heat and drought, but are best when grown for a spring or fall crop. The mild-flavored leaves can be harvested at any

Above: Okra 'Clemson Spineless'
Right: Mustard greens 'Burpee's Fordhook® Fancy'

time for salads or cooking. These plants have no significant pests or diseases. Burpee's 'Fordhook® Fancy' is early to harvest—40 days—with deeply curled and fringed leaves that curl back like ostrich plumes; the variety is slow to bolt.

Cultural Information: Grow mustard greens in loamy, fertile soil. Sow seeds ½ inch deep. Mature plants should stand 8 inches apart. Water well during dry spells. Cold weather and light frosts will improve the flavor. Where winters are mild, plant in late summer and for harvest through fall and into winter. (See "Planting Guide for Leafy Greens," page 42.)

Harvest: Start harvesting as soon as there is enough for a meal. They can be harvested at any time and at any size; from 6 to 8 inches is standard harvest size. The lower leaves may be harvested continuously, or the plant can be harvested all at once.

Okra Mallow Family Easy ○

Days to Harvest: 50 to 55
Days to Germinate: 4 to 14
Temperature to Germinate: 68 to 86 degrees Fahrenheit
Temperature for Growth: 70 to 80 degrees Fahrenheit
Height: 2 to 7 feet
Characteristics: Related to cotton and hibiscus, okra is ornamental in the back of the flower border. It thrives in warm weather and is grown for its immature pods which add body and flavor when cut up in soups, stews, catsup and relishes. Also delicious as a cooked vegetable, its texture is improved by cooking with vinegar. 'Clemson Spineless' is the favorite, an abundant

producer with dark green, slightly grooved, pointed, straight, spineless pods.

Cultural Information: Okra likes a well-limed, fertile, light soil with a pH of 7.0-8.0. Have your soil tested to be sure of the pH. Delay seeding until after the last frost and the weather is consistently warm. Two or three side-dressings of well-rotted manure or a complete, slow-release fertilizer will keep the plants bearing all summer. Water well if hot, dry weather persists.

Harvest: Pick every two or three days for a continuous harvest. Pods are best when young. Older pods can be used for decoration.

Onions Amaryllis Family Easy ○

Days to Harvest: from sets, 85 days; from seeds, 95–125 days
Days to Germinate: 6 to 10
Temperature to Germinate: 68 to 70 degrees Fahrenheit
Growth Temperature: 55 to 70 degrees Fahrenheit
Height: 10 inches
Characteristics: Meals would be so much less tasty were it not for the onion and its companions, the scallion, the shallot, the leek, and the garlic bulb. Without them, we would all miss the special piquant flavors that enliven our meals, day in, day out. Onions grow and store easily, and are a good source of healthy vitamins like A and C. They also produce a high yield for the little space they use.

Most vegetables are annuals, but onions and their relations are actually biennials, going to seed their second summer. We harvest and eat them before they have a chance to set seed. During their first growing season,

onions store food in enlarged, modified stem structures—actually leaf bases compressed into a tight bulb—so they can produce flowers and seeds in their second year. At the end of that first growing season, the tight bulbs are large enough to eat and consequently, we grow onions as annuals (this is the case with garlic, shallots, and leeks, too).

Cultural Information: Onions are classified as short-day or long-day varieties. Short-day varieties such as the Bermudas grow well in the South. Farther north, the longer-day varieties, such as the yellow globes, requiring 14 to 16 hours of daylight, are the best growers and producers. For best results, use onion plants or sets for your initial efforts in growing onions. Onions from seed should be started 8 to 10 weeks before transplant date. Trim the tops if they get too long, to promote root development. When transplanting onions into the garden, trim any tops that flop over and rest on the soil (where they can pick up disease). Tops should stand tall.

Onions require both cool and hot temperatures; in cool weather, they grow their tops, and in warm weather they form and enlarge their bulbs. They also require reasonably fertile soil, well prepared with lime and slow-release 5–10–5 fertilizer. Remove all stones and sticks to ensure good root development.

Onions (along with family members garlic, shallots, scallions, and leeks) grow well in rich, loose soil. Sandy loam and peat soil are best. These heavy feeders appreciate a complete slow-release fertilizer (5–10–5) in spring, worked in about a week before planting.

It is important to keep weeds under control throughout the growing season. With their thin leaf stalks and shallow roots, onions have trouble competing for nutrients, space, and sunlight with vigorous weeds. A

ONION VARIETIES*

LONG-DAY TYPES FOR NORTHERN GARDENS	FLAVOR	SIZE AND SHAPE	KEEPING QUALITY	NOTES
Burpee 'Sweet Spanish Hybrid'	Mild	Large globe	Fairly good	Spanish types are especially good in arid parts of the West but are widely adapted throughout the United States.
'Spanish Yellow Hybrid' (from plants)	Mild	Large globe	Fairly good	
'Sweet Spanish' (Yellow Utah)	Mild	Large globe	Fair	
'White Sweet Spanish'	Mild	Large globe	Poor	
'Burpee Yellow Globe Hybrid'	Fairly strong	Medium globe	Outstanding	Especially good in the Northeast
'Sweet Sandwich'	Fairly strong	Medium globe	Very good	Gets milder in storage
'Bermuda White Hybrid' (from plants)	Very mild	Large semiflat	Fair	
'Giant Red Hamburger' (from plants)	Fairly mild	Large semiflat	Good	
Yellow onions from sets	Fairly strong	Large globe	Very good	
White onions from sets	Mild	Large globe	Fairly good	
SHORT-DAY TYPE FOR THE SOUTH				
'Granex Yellow Hybrid'	Very mild	Large flat	Fair	
ONIONS FOR NORTH AND SOUTH				
'Evergreen Long White Bunching'	Mild	Does not bulb	Poor	Can be wintered over successfully
'Crystal Wax Pickling PRR'	Mild	Small globe	Poor	For "pearl" onions

*Please check your most recent Burpee catalog for current listings.

Onion 'Burpee Yellow Globe Hybrid'

Parsnip 'Hollow Crown'

Snap pea 'Sugar Bon'

Snap pea 'Snappy'

light mulch will help check weeds. Onions like a soil to be slightly acid, about 5.8 to 6.5 on the pH scale. They can be grown from seed, transplants or sets, all readily available from seed catalogs or garden centers. Onions are subject to few diseases and are ignored by most pests.

Harvest: When the bulbs are ready, the tops begin to yellow and fall over. To harvest your crop all at once, break the remaining upright tops with a rake or by hand and leave the plants in the ground until all the tops are dead. Then pull all the plants and spread them in the sun for three or four days to dry, with the tops covering the bulbs. When the bulbs are dry, cut each top off about 1 inch from the bulb. Store in mesh bags in a cool, dry location. They'll last through the winter.

Parsnips Parsley Family Easy ○

Days to Harvest: 105 to 150
Days to Germinate: 6 to 28
Temperature to Germinate: 68 to 86 degrees Fahrenheit
Growth Temperature: 60 to 70 degrees Fahrenheit
Height: 10 to 15 feet
Characteristics: Before potatoes were popular, parsnips were the garden staple. The roots are nutritious and particularly delicious late in fall, after frost adds sweetness. Enjoy parsnips grilled, sautéed, puréed or mashed with potatoes. Parsnips resemble carrots, except they are cream-colored and have rougher skin. You can steam fresh parsnips in their skins, then peel them if you like. They're delicious served with butter, wonderful

served pan-glazed like sweet potatoes. 'Hollow Crown' is a variety grown for its heavy yield of roots, 12 inches long, 2¾ inches thick at the top, and free from side roots.

Cultural Information: Parsnips are slow to germinate. Sow 1 inch deep in fertile soil that has been prepared 12 to 18 inches deep. Remove sticks and stones before planting to ensure development of straight, vigorous roots. Thin to 4 to 6 inches apart.

Planted in the spring, parsnips aren't ready to harvest until after the first fall frost. Freezing doesn't hurt the roots. Dig them as needed or leave them for an early spring treat. The young sprouts are slow to break ground and the young plants are weak and need protection from encroaching weeds. Once established, they need little care. They need 105 days or more to mature, and require more room than carrots; their roots are sometimes 15 inches deep and the plants grow to about 24 inches tall.

Harvest: For best flavor, don't harvest until after frost. Store, roots and all, in moist containers of sand or leave in the ground. In areas of cold winters, protect with a pile of leaves or hay; harvest in March before new spring growth begins.

Peas Pea Family Easy ○

Days to Harvest: 55 to 80
Days to Germinate: 5 to 8
Temperature to Germinate: 68 degrees Fahrenheit
Growth Temperature: 65 to 70 degrees Fahrenheit
Height: 18 inches to 16 feet
Characteristics: Earliest of the

garden vegetables to go into the ground at planting time, peas are cool-weather lovers and will not tolerate midsummer heat. The three types of peas are green peas (also called garden peas or English peas), snow peas (also known as sugar peas or Chinese pea pods), and snap peas, a relative newcomer to the pea family.

Green peas are grown for their mature seeds (the peas) and the pods are usually discarded. Snow peas are grown for their tender, succulent young pods, familiar from Chinese cooking. Snap peas are delicious, tender, and sweet at any stage, eaten pods and all when the seeds are full size. There are bush-type plants which grow to be 1½ to 2 feet tall; vine types which, like beans, are more prolific but take longer to mature, and tall plants that need support to keep the harvest off the ground.

In the North, peas are sown as both a spring and fall crop. If summers are cool, they are grown from spring right through fall. In the South and Gulf Coast states, peas are grown in the fall, winter, and early spring. 'Burpeeana Early', 63 days, is Burpee's extremely prolific, early, deliciously sweet, all-purpose pea. 'Maestro' is another early variety, 61 days, disease-resistant and recommended for fall crops. 'Oregon Sugar Pod II', 68 days, is a good disease-resistant snow pea, and 'Sugar Snap®', 70 days, is a #1 All-Time, All-American Vegetable Award winner.

Cultural Information: For the earliest possible spring planting, it's best to thoroughly prepare the garden bed the preceding fall. As soon as the ground thaws in the spring, sow the seeds. (Because the soil will still be damp, try to choose a spot near the edge of your garden so you can stand outside the garden to sow seeds without stepping on the soil and compacting it.) Simply push the seeds down into the soil with your fingers and sprinkle with a soil inoculant like Burpee Booster for Peas and Beans, which puts nitrogen-fixing bacteria into the soil. These bacteria help peas use free atmospheric nitrogen. It improves the growth of plants, increases crop yields and puts nitrogen back into the soil where it can be used by the next crop. This method of sowing will not damage the soil structure as long as you do not work the soil again while it is wet. Working the soil while it is wet can compact it and cause lasting damage.

For high yields, especially with the low-growing bush types, try growing your peas the way commercial growers do: Prepare a bed 3 to 5 feet wide and as long as you wish. Broadcast the seeds, tossing them lightly over the soil surface. Draw a cultivator or a rake through the soil to cover the seeds. The loss in yields from seeds that remain exposed is negligible. Because they are grown so thickly, the plants will support themselves and act as a living mulch, keeping the ground cool and moist. With this method, your harvest yield will be very high.

When planting fall crops, plant 60 to 70 days before the date of the first expected fall frost. If you are looking for a continuous spring harvest, plant early, midseason, and late varieties at the same time. This will allow all three types to take advantage of the cool weather. Snap peas are especially vigorous, usually growing to more than 6 feet high. Burpee customers have reported plants of 10 feet and more, so provide good support for the tall and climbing varieties.

One of the most common problems is root damage from too-deep cultivation. Cultivate carefully or pile mulch or loose soil up around base of plants to inhibit weeds. Aphids and peaweevils can be a problem. To control peaweevils, practice crop rotation, cultivate the soil thoroughly between crop plantings and keep weeds down.

Harvest: When harvesting peas, use one hand to steady the plant, the other to pull the pods carefully. This avoids accidentally uprooting the plants. Harvest green peas when the pods are well-filled, but before they harden and fade in color. That way, they will be sweet and tender. The sugar content of green peas decreases rapidly after picking, so pick them just before you need them. Peas used immediately after picking for eating, canning, or freezing will retain their sweetness very well.

Snow peas are best harvested when the pods are long and seeds just starting to fill out. Pick frequently—daily, when possible—to prevent them from developing large seeds and fibrous pods. If some pods become overmature, shell and cook them like green peas. Snow peas keep better than green peas and can be kept in the refrigerator for up to ten days without ap-

preciable loss in quality. Excellent stir-fried, steamed, or prepared like snap beans.

Snap peas are best when the pods are 2½ to 3 inches long and plump with mature peas. The pod walls grow sweeter as the peas develop, but harvest them before the pods become over-mature. Lots of people like to eat snap peas raw, in salads, or right off the vine. They are delicious cooked and served like snap beans. Whole pods freeze well, but use frozen pods in hot dishes only because they lose their crunchiness. After the harvest, till the plants back into the soil or add them to the compost

Drying Beans and Peas

Because legumes are an excellent source of protein, you may want to store them for winter use. They will have to be dried. The procedure is easy.

Leave the pods of the beans or peas on the plant until partially dry. Then pull up the plants and hang them in a warm, dry, well-ventilated place until thoroughly dry. The skin of the pod shrinks and takes on a papery look. The bean silhouette becomes more visible. Shell them, place on a cookie sheet, and dry in a 135 degree Fahrenheit oven for 3 to 4 hours. Let the seeds cool to room temperature, then store in an airtight container in a cool place.

They're ready to use when you're ready to use them. Use this technique to dry the following:

Black Turtle
California Blackeye
Dwarf Horticultural
Dwarf Taylor
Fava
Garbanzo
Great Northern
Maine Yellow Eye
Mung
Navy
Pinto
Purple Hull
Red Kidney
Red Kloud
Soldier
Swedish Brown
White Kidney
White Marrow

Snow pea 'Mammoth Melting Sugar'

pile. They're great nitrogen contributors to your garden.

Pea, Blackeye; see *Beans, Cowpea*

Pea, Crowder; see *Beans, Cowpea*

CAUTION: If you're growing both sweet and hot pepper varieties, be sure to label carefully. Both pepper plants and their fruits tend to look alike, and you don't want any surprises at harvest.

Pepper 'Super Chili'

The most popular—and trouble-free—way to store hot peppers is to dry them. String mature red peppers by piercing the cap or calyx with a needle and heavy thread. Hang in a warm, dry, well-ventilated, dark or shaded place (not in the sun) to dry. They make a colorful addition to your kitchen; hang dried peppers in a handy spot, and whenever you need one, just pull it from the string. Hot peppers remain hot, even after they are dried. In recipes, a touch of hot pepper goes a long, long way.

CAUTION: Hot peppers can burn skin on contact, and fumes from chopping or cooking them can irritate the lungs or eyes. When harvesting or preparing hot peppers, it is recommended that you wear rubber gloves. Always wash your hands thoroughly with soap and water after handling hot peppers, and never touch your face, especially your eyes.

Pea, Southern; see *Beans, Cowpea*

Peas, Chick; see *Beans*

Peppers Nightshade Family
Easy ○

Days to Harvest: 60 to 100*
Days to Germinate: 6 to 14
Temperature to Germinate: 68 to 86 degrees Fahrenheit
Growth Temperature: 65 to 75 degrees Fahrenheit
Height: 2½ feet
Characteristics: Grow peppers just the way you like them. For sweet, grow the familiar bell, 'Sweet Banana' or 'Sweet Cherry'. For hot, grow chili, cayenne, and hot cherry types. ("Hot" peppers vary quite a lot in their "hotness," so check the descriptions in your seed catalog or on the seed packet. Even then, you'll find that "hotness" can vary from one pepper to another, grown on the same plant.)

A number of colorful types will add an appealing look to your table. Some varieties, in fact, make very pretty additions to your flower border, and you can save space in your vegetable garden by growing them like flowers in the flower garden. 'Crispy Hybrid' will give you a heavy crop of delicious bell peppers all season. 'Gypsy Hybrid' is very early—65 days—with sweet, tapered fruits. 'New Ace Hybrid' is a dark green, stuffing-type pepper, and a good choice for northern regions and for the greenhouse.

Cultural Information: Pepper seeds take a little longer than tomatoes or eggplant to become seedlings, so you must start them indoors about eight to ten weeks before the last expected spring frost. Plant in well-

drained, sandy loam. "Side-dress" once or twice during the growing season. Keep watered and mulch to conserve moisture. Peppers germinate and grow much as tomatoes and eggplant, except for those two extra weeks from seed planting to transplanting.

When transplanting pepper plants, place them 18 to 24 inches apart in rows 2 to 3 feet apart.

The most common pests are aphids, stalk borers, cutworms and tomato hornworms. Common diseases are anthracnose and leaf spots. Blossom drop may occur if the temperature falls below 55 degrees Fahrenheit; when blossoms fall off, the plant doesn't set fruit. Extended rainy or cool periods also may cause blossom drop. Fortunately, blossom drop is a temporary condition that is corrected when temperature/weather returns to normal. Blossom end rot, caused by a calcium deficiency in the soil, may also occur; black, dry, or sunken spots appear, usually starting at the blossom end of fruit, and fruits often ripen prematurely. Solutions are to apply lime to the soil each spring before planting, avoid uneven water absorption by mulching and regular watering, avoid high-nitrogen fertilizer and improve soil drainage with compost or other organic materials. Curled or twisted top growth may occur if herbicide was applied somewhere in the area. This can cause fruit deformities and sometimes mottling of leaves, which can lead to a viral disease.

Holes in ripening fruit may be caused by pheasants or other birds, turtles, or mice. Sunscald

—yellowish or whitish patches that appear on the side of the fruit that faces the sun, turning to blisters with a paperlike surface—occurs when plants have suddenly lost foliage due to overpruning or leaf diseases. Avoid excessive pruning; cover exposed fruits with cheesecloth or straw. Wilting may occur if the soil is either too dry or waterlogged. Keep soil evenly moist throughout the growing season.
Harvest: Peppers can be picked anytime after they reach full size whether they're green, red, or "breaking" (part green, part red). Cut the pepper from the plant using a sharp knife or pruning shears, leaving a small part of the stem attached to each fruit. Sweet bell, pimento, and cherry peppers are delicious eaten green, but are sweeter and higher in vitamins if allowed to turn bright red before harvesting (some varieties are golden-yellow at maturity). 'Sweet Banana' peppers mature from green through yellow and red.

Hot peppers may be harvested at any stage, with the exception of 'Jalapeno M' and 'Anaheim TMR 23', which are picked green. Cayenne types are picked when they are red. Bell peppers can be chopped and quick-frozen for use in many recipes; sweet cherry and banana peppers and hot cherry peppers are perfect for pickling.

Potatoes (Irish or White) Nightshade Family Easy ○
Days to Harvest: 80 to 120
Days to sprout from eyes: 110 to 140
Temperature to Germinate: 65 to 72
Growth Temperature: 65 to 75

Height: 1½ to 2 feet
Characteristics: New potatoes, harvested in summer shortly after the plants flower and served garden-fresh, have a wonderful and distinctive taste that can't be matched by "boughten" potatoes. This is reason enough to grow potatoes yourself.
Note: potatoes can be poisonous! The green parts of potatoes —especially the skin when it has been exposed to sunlight, and all potato sprouts—contain concentrated amounts of solanine, an alkaloid toxic to animals and humans. This is why it is important to keep potato tubers out of sunlight at all times. Keep the following in mind:

1. You can cook and eat the white flesh of sun-greened potatoes after you have peeled them and cut away all green parts.
2. You can cook and eat potatoes which have sprouted after you have removed all sprouts.
3. Be sure to discard all sprouts and green peelings where animals won't find and eat them.
4. Never feed greened potatoes, spoiled potatoes, sprouts, peelings, or plants to livestock, poultry, or pets.

For baking, grow 'Acadia Russet' with its elongated, oval tubers. 'Kennebec' is an all-purpose potato with smooth-textured, white flesh and shallow eyes. 'Red Pontiac' is rosy skinned, an all-purpose potato that does well in heavy soils. 'Yukon Gold' is a true taste treat with yellow skin and yellow flesh.
Cultural Information: As soon as you can work your garden in the spring, it's time to plant

potatoes. This will likely be a month or so before your last frost, when the ground is dry enough to dig.

Grow them in a location where potatoes, tomatoes, strawberries, or eggplants were not grown the year before. The soil should be light, well drained, and acid with a pH of 4.8 to 5.4. Avoid planting in an area with freshly turned grass sod. If your soil is heavy clay, work in plenty of organic matter.

Don't plant potatoes from food markets. Chances are they have been sprayed to slow sprouting. When you buy seed potatoes from a reliable seed supplier, they are certified disease-free, coated with lime for spoilage control, and packed in vermiculite, which controls the moisture level and insulates the eyes from damage.

Potatoes are traditionally planted by burying sets, sections with eyes, in a few inches of soil and hilling up additional soil or mulch around them, or by laying the eyes on the soil surface and covering them with black plastic. Whole potatoes can be planted to produce more —but smaller—plants. The first

Pepper 'Mexi Bell Hybrid'

Potatoes 'Kennebec' (top) and 'Red Pontiac' (bottom)

Uncle Gideon's
Quick Lunch Potato.

Below: Pumpkin 'Jack Be Little'

Right: Pumpkin 'Spirit Hybrid'

method is more productive. Turn the soil to a depth of about 12 inches and plant the rows 2 to 3 feet apart.

You can hasten the rooting and the maturing process through a procedure called "chitting." That simply means you spread the seed potatoes in a sunny indoor place for two or three weeks prior to planting. It takes the eyes from dormant to growing shoots.

To plant, dig a furrow 3 to 4 inches deep and lay an inch or so of compost, dried or well-rotted manure or slow-release 5–10–10 fertilizer and mix it with the soil in the furrow. Set the seed pieces about 10 inches apart in rows 2 to 3 feet apart, cut side down so the eyes face up, and press them firmly into the soil. Cover with about 3 inches of loose soil and pat it down slightly with the back of your hoe. When the seedlings and leaves appear, hill up some loose soil around the stems, but leave at least 4 inches of stem and leaves uncovered.

If you plan to grow them under black plastic mulch, be sure the summers are not too hot, since plastic will warm the soil too. Cover the rows with black plastic mulch, burying the edges in soil to hold it in place. Cut through the mulch at 9- to 12-inch intervals and open holes 3 to 4 inches deep. A trowel works well for cutting the mulch as well as digging the holes. Work in some slow-release 5–10–10 fertilizer or well rotted compost at the bottom of each hole and drop in the potato section, eyes up.

Common pests and diseases are the Colorado potato beetle, fleabeetle, leafhoppers and aphids, soil insects (wireworms, white grubs, and cutworms), potato blight, verticillium wilt and scab disease.
Harvest: You can harvest mature potatoes conventionally, after the tops have died back. Store in a cool (35 to 50 degrees Fahrenheit), damp, dark place. Or you can "rob" a hill in midsummer, by feeling gently under the soil at the base of the plants and removing the small, hard potatoes. If you take only one potato from each plant, you'll enjoy a special treat without harming your fall harvest.

Pumpkin Gourd Family Easy ○

Days to Harvest: 90 to 120
Days to Germinate: 4 to 7
Temperature to Germinate: 68 to 86 degrees Fahrenheit
Growth Temperature: 75 to 80 degrees Fahrenheit
Height: 12 to 18 inches
Characteristics: Think of pumpkins as large, round winter squash. Pumpkin flesh is delicious puréed and used in soups, pies, bread, cakes, cookies, and muffins. The purée can be canned or frozen and stored for use throughout the year.

If you're working with a small garden and must conserve space, try planting pumpkins such as Burpee's 'Triple Treat' (6 to 8 pounds each) which are good for carving and pies. Hull-less seeds make delicious snacks.

Pumpkins, because they are late-maturing, can be planted near crops that will be harvested earlier (early corn, for example) to conserve garden space; by the time the early crop has been harvested, the pumpkins will be ready to spread out. Smaller pumpkin varieties can be grown on a fence or trellis.

If you want to show off, or enter competitions, plant 'Prizewinner Pumpkin'. Allow the first female flower (and possibly the second) to be pollinated and begin developing, then pinch off all the subsequent female flowers. You want only one pumpkin to a vine, but make sure it has a good start before pinching other flowers off. Plan to leave room around the plants. Pumpkins have grown to over 400 pounds. We recommend using plastic mulch to grow pumpkins; it traps warmth in the soil, smothers weeds, conserves moisture, and protects the fruit from contact with the ground where it can pick up bacteria and insects. (See "Planting Guide for Vine Crops," page 55.)
Cultural Information: Pumpkins have a vining habit and bear separate male and female flowers. They are planted in hills

(clusters—see page 79) and grow like other vine crops. Most varieties require a great deal of growing space, although some newer varieties grow in a bush-like habit and require only about 9 square feet per plant.

For common pests and diseases, see Cucumbers.

Harvest: Pumpkins should be harvested when the rinds are hard and are a deep, solid orange; they must be harvested before they are injured by the first heavy frost.

For storage, leave 3 to 4 inches of stem attached to the fruit and cure at a temperature of 75 to 80 degrees Fahrenheit for one or two weeks. After curing, store in a cool, dry, well-ventilated place at 50 to 65 degrees Fahrenheit.

All pumpkin seeds are edible and very nutritious. Some have seed coats, some are "naked." To prepare for eating, scoop them out of the pumpkin and wash them lightly to separate them from the fibers (or, pick them clean by hand). Spread out the seeds on paper towels or plates and let them dry for a few days in a warm, dry, well-ventilated place.

Radish Parsley Family Easy
○

Days to Harvest: 22 to 55, depending on variety
Days to Germinate: 4 to 6
Temperature to Germinate: 45 degrees Fahrenheit all-season types, 55 degrees fall and winter types
Growth Temperature: 70 degrees Fahrenheit
Height: 4 to 6 inches
Characteristics: Radishes are the gardener's handy man. They

grow fast, maturing in 30 days or so, and can be planted anywhere in the garden. They are frequently grown in flower beds, or sown together with slow-germinating varieties (carrots, beets, parsley, and parsnips) to mark the rows. In summer, growing radishes break the soil crust, making life easier for the later sprouts, and the picking of radishes helps aerate the soil and makes more room for the companion crop. The shallow roots of radishes will not interfere with the other crops, and they are usually harvested before the room they use is needed for the other crop.

Burpee divides radish varieties into three types: early or spring radishes, all-season radishes, and fall and winter radishes. Early radishes are those most familiar in markets and the most common ones in home gardens. They include the red globe-type (like 'Champion' and 'Cherry Belle'), the long, white types ('Burpee White' and 'White Icicle') and the bicolor varieties ('Sparkler' and 'French Breakfast'). They are the quickest to grow, maturing in three to four weeks. For a continuous crop, sow them every seven to ten days from early spring. You can make a final sowing a month before the first fall frost for a late crop. Sow them near the surface, because deep sowing will elongate the roots.

In frost-free areas (Zones 9 and 10), sow early radishes from fall to spring. Early varieties are also adapted for greenhouse use in winter. These radishes, being fairly small and quick to mature, are ideal for growing in all kinds of outdoor containers, including window boxes.

Radishes 'White Icicle', 'Cherry Belle', and 'French Breakfast'

All-season radishes mature in about 45 days, are white and grow quite long without getting pithy or strong-flavored. They withstand heat better than the other types, extending the spring growing season into summer, and they do very well as a fall/winter crop.

Fall/winter radishes are best known in the Orient. They need cool weather at the end of their growing season. Sow in mid-summer for late fall and winter use. The roots can be mild (try 'Summer Cross') or pungent ('All Seasons White'), according to the variety, and they come in various shapes and colors. Many grow quite large, often with several inches of root showing above the ground.

Cultural Information: Plant radishes in a loamy soil, free of rocks and stones that can cause misshapen roots. If you plant in a raised bed or double-dig your bed, you will produce superior radishes. In raised beds, sow seeds in rows 2 inches apart; elsewhere sow in double rows 6 inches apart with a foot between each set of rows. Sow seeds ⅓ inch deep with three seeds per inch of row. When plants are half grown, thin them so there are 12 to 18 plants per foot of row.

Harvest: Radishes are best picked within a few days of reaching maturity. They stay crisp in the refrigerator only a few days.

Rhubarb
Buckwheat Family Moderately Difficult ○ ◐

Days to Germinate: 7 to 21
Temperature to Germinate: 68 to 86 degrees Fahrenheit
Growth Temperature: No higher than 90 degrees Fahrenheit
Height: 18 to 36 inches
Years to Harvest: second year after planting
Characteristics: Originally a Siberian plant, rhubarb was introduced into Europe over three hundred years ago. It is valued in spring for its stems which, when cooked and sweetened, are a delicious substitute for later-blooming fruit. Rhubarb can be a dramatic accent for the back of the flower border, for its large leaves, red stalks, and unusual flowers. The leaves, containing calcium oxalate, are poisonous, and should not be eaten. The plants are perennial and will return each year with minimum maintenance and abundant harvest. The stalks are delicious stewed, alone or with strawberries, and in pies, pastries and cobblers—a great spring treat.

Rhubarb 'MacDonald'

One of the best varieties is 'MacDonald', with brilliant red color. 'Victoria' is a good green variety shaded with red.
Cultural Information: Rhubarb thrives in cool weather and is poorly suited to southern climates. In early spring, set roots 3 to 4 feet apart in well-prepared, enriched soil. The crowns or tops should be covered lightly and the area around the plant top-dressed with well-rotted manure or compost. Fertilize every spring. The flower stalks need to be removed as they appear so as not to deplete the plant's energy. Water well during dry periods. The roots furnish a modest cutting of stalks just one year from planting, and produce abundantly thereafter.

Rhubarb plants are easily propagated in the spring: Lift the root and divide it into pieces. Each piece must contain one or more buds. Plants can remain without dividing for twenty years or longer but will have better flavor and performance if divided and replanted in enriched soil every ten years.
Harvest: Grow one year before harvest. Harvest individual stalks, tenderest when the size of celery ribs. To harvest, grasp the larger outside stalks firmly near the base and pull. Red-stalked rhubarb is sweetest, preferred for freezing and canning. CAUTION: The leaves are poisonous.

Roquette; see *Garden rocket*

Rugula; see *Garden rocket*

Rutabaga
(Swedish Turnips, Canadian Turnips, Yellow Turnips) Parsley Family Moderate ○

Days to Harvest: 80 to 90
Days to Germinate: 3 to 14
Temperature to Germinate: 68 to 86
Growth Temperature: 50 to 75 degrees Fahrenheit
Height: 12 inches
Characteristics: Rutabagas are similar to turnips but more flavorful. They also carry more vitamins and retain their food value longer in storage. 'Burpee's Purple-Top Yellow' is sweet, fine-grained with yellow flesh that turns bright orange when cooked.
Cultural Information: Rutabagas are best grown as a fall crop, for they prefer cool weather. They are slower-growing than turnips. Sow seeds from early to midsummer, allowing 90 days to maturity. They don't like extreme hot weather, so in the South and other hot-weather areas, sow turnips instead. Harvest the roots when they are about 3 inches across.
Harvest: Rutabagas are frost-hardy and can be left in the ground all winter, to be dug as needed or stored as recommended for other root crops (see page 48). They keep well in winter storage.

Shallots
Amaryllis Family Easy ○

Days to Harvest: 30 to 40 for green tops
Characteristics: Shallots are better known in Europe than in America. Because they are often hard to find here, it's especially nice to grow them in your garden. Shallots have a mild, onionlike flavor that adds wonderful bouquet to delicate sauces that would otherwise be overpowered by onions and garlic. The bulbs look like little brown

or purple onions; they grow in clusters at the base of the plant.
Cultural Information: Separate the little bulbs before planting, and set them about 6 inches apart in rows 1½ feet apart, as each bulb will form a whole clump. Water well after planting; when they have established themselves, give them about half as much water as you would give onions. Like other members of the onion family, shallots like plenty of fertilizer. They are generally grown, harvested, cured, and stored like onions, although the bulbs may be left in the ground to overwinter under a layer of mulch. In the South, shallots are sometimes grown for their green leaves rather than the dried bulbs. Sets are planted in fall (late enough so they won't put out any top growth that would be damaged over the winter) and harvested during the winter. Shallots are generally pest- and disease-free.
Harvest: See Onions.

Spinach Goosefoot Family Easy ○

Days to Harvest: 40 to 50
Days to Germinate: 7 to 21
Temperature to Germinate: 59 degrees Fahrenheit
Growth Temperature: 75 degrees Fahrenheit
Height: 10 to 12 inches
Characteristics: Dark green, delicious leaves make spinach a popular home garden crop. The plants are relatively carefree. There are many different varieties, with leaves from the heavily savoyed, to semi-crinkled, to smooth.

In general, the crop does not do well in summer heat and longer daylight hours, which trigger the plants to produce seed. (When plants rapidly and prematurely turn most of their energy to producing seed, it's called bolting.) For spring planting, choose heat-resistant varieties like 'Avon Hybrid', a quick-growing variety with large, succulent, dark green, semi-crinkled leaves that are easy to clean, or 'Bloomsdale Long-Standing' with its heavy yield of thick-textured, very crinkled, glossy dark green leaves. When you grow in summer heat, it's wise to select varieties that are mildew-resistant too. Consider such hot-weather spinach "substitutes" as Swiss Chard, New Zealand spinach, and tampala.
Cultural Information: For best germination soak the seeds in lukewarm water for a few hours before sowing. Sow the seeds and grow the plants as you would lettuce. Spinach likes soil on the sour side, with a pH between 6 and 7. "Side-dress" when plants are one-third grown and keep them well-watered. (See "Planting Guide for Leafy Greens," page 42.)
Harvest: Spinach can be harvested at any time. When the leaves are fully expanded, you may pick the large, outer leaves only, allowing the centers of the plants to produce more leaves, or you can cut the plants off at ground level.

Spinach beet; see *Swiss chard*

Squash Gourd Family Easy ○

Days to Harvest: Summer, 50 to 60; Winter, 80 to 120; Bush types, 75
Days to Germinate: 4 to 7
Temperature to Germinate: 68 to 86 degrees Fahrenheit

Growth Temperature: 70 to 85 degrees Fahrenheit
Height: Bush types are 2½ feet tall, vines can be 6 feet
Characteristics: Squash is a Native American plant that thrives almost anywhere in the United States where there is adequate moisture. There are many varieties, but they belong to only three different species.
General Cultural Information: Squash need fertile soil with lots of organic matter and good drainage. Use plastic mulch to conserve moisture, warm the soil and keep fruit clean and disease-free. Squash are heat-loving vegetables and shouldn't be planted until a week or longer after the last frost date in your area, so the soil will be sufficiently warm.

Growing squash (except bush types) takes a large space in the vegetable garden. We recommend sowing in hills (see page 79) as in the sowing of pumpkins. Don't thin seedlings too quickly; make sure they are well established. They will need 6 to 8 feet in all directions to have room to scramble and grow. Water deeply and don't worry if the leaves wilt in the hot midday sun as long as they revive in the evening. Side-dress when plants start to run at blossom start.

Nearly all vine crops produce male and female flowers on each plant, although male flowers are predominant. The first flowers to appear will be male. Frequently gardeners worry unnecessarily about this when they observe that no fruit is setting. But as in most things, patience will prevail, as a little later female flowers do develop and fruit begins to grow.

Rutabaga 'Burpee's Purple-Top Yellow'

Shallot

Spinach 'Tyee Hybrid'

Female flowers are distinguished from male flowers by the tiny fruit buds at the base of the petals on the female flower. When pollination occurs, these are the buds that develop into mature fruit.

If you want to be sure that the first female flowers on a vine plant produce fruit, try this simple method of pollination. Break off a newly opened male flower in the morning and rub the pollen-laden stamen or spur in the center of the flower around the inside of a newly opened female flower.

Squash suffer from many of the same pests and disease problems as cucumbers. (See "Planting Guide for Vine Crops," pages 55–56.)

WINTER SQUASH

Winter squash, traditionally eaten only when fully matured, may be stored for several months. Some better-known types are: butternut, buttercup, acorn, hubbard, spaghetti and, yes, pumpkin. Newer winter squash varieties are available that can be eaten young like summer squash or left on the vine to mature. Winter squash are most commonly baked, but many varieties can be puréed and used to make pumpkin pie. You can batter-dip and fry male squash flowers, or stuff the blossoms with meat, fish, crumb, or cheese stuffings. Burpee's 'Butterbush' is space-saving and quick to mature (75 days); this is the first bush-type butternut squash, introduced in 1978. Considered a low-calorie substitute for spaghetti or noodles, spaghetti squash is a popular winter squash with spaghetti-like flesh. When preparing spaghetti squash for the table, punch one or two small holes in the fruit with a metal skewer, then boil the whole squash for 30 minutes (or bake it at 350 degrees Fahrenheit for an hour). When the squash yields to medium pressure, it's done. Cut in half lengthwise, and scoop out and discard the seeds. Pull the flesh into "spaghetti" strands by dragging a fork back and forth across the surface. Put in a bowl and toss gently. Cooked strands may be served like pasta, tossed with butter and grated Parmesan cheese or topped with sauce. They can also be chilled and added to salads.

Harvest: Winter squash are ready for harvest when they have turned a solid color and the rind is hard. Many gardeners like to harvest winter squash after a light frost has killed the vines (some say it makes them more flavorful) but care must be taken to harvest before a hard frost.

Acorn squash should be harvested when the spot touching the ground turns a yellowish orange. For best results, cut the fruit from the vine, leaving about 2 inches of the stem attached. Bruised or immature fruit will not store well and should be used as soon as possible. After harvest, winter squash should be cured for a week or two at temperatures of 75 to 80 degrees Fahrenheit to harden the shell, then stored in a cool, dry place with a temperature range of 50 to 55 degrees Fahrenheit. Burpee's 'Bush Table Queen' is a bush type acorn squash that is very productive in a small space.

Spaghetti squash are ready for harvest when they've turned from green to yellow. At that time they are about 8 to 10 inches long and weigh 3 to 6 pounds.

Spaghetti squash should be harvested with an inch of stem attached to the fruit. Cure outdoors in a sunny spot for about a week, then store in a cool, dry place.

SUMMER SQUASH

Zucchini are good when grated and baked in breads, steamed quickly in butter, sliced raw into salads, baked and stuffed whole, puréed in soups, or added to stir-fries. Large zucchini (8 inches and larger) are especially recommended for soups and baking. 'Burpee Hybrid Zucchini' and 'Butterstick Hybrid' are recommended for their heavy yield and excellent flavor.

Crookneck and straightneck squash can be sliced in half, steamed in butter, and sprinkled with nutmeg for a tasty side dish. Patty pan types are particularly delicious when stuffed, with meat, breadcrumbs, or rice. 'Pic N' Pic' is a heavy producer of tender crookneck squash over a long period.

Harvest: Summer squash should be harvested young and is best eaten within a few days of harvesting. Patty pans are at their best when 2 to 4 inches in diameter; the other summer squashes are at their peak when 6 to 8 inches long (larger, they tend to be tough). Frequent harvesting encourages continuous fruit production. When zucchini is 6 inches or less in length is the ideal time to harvest. If you leave mature fruits on the plants, subsequent fruit production will be slow.

Sugarhat chicory; see
Chicory

Sweet Potato Morning Glory
Family Moderate ○
Days to Harvest: 90 to 120
Growth Temperature: 77 degrees
Fahrenheit plus
Height: 18 inches
Characteristics: The sweet potato, like corn, was a regional staple of Native American diets. Oddly enough, sweet potatoes are very popular in Japan and carry twice the food value of white rice. They are attractive in the garden for their petunia-like flowers and foliage. Sweet potatoes are of two types, producing tuberous roots with either dry or moist flesh. The most commonly grown are the moist types, which are sometimes called "yams." They have copper or reddish skins and delicious, sweet, deep orange flesh. The true yam is an entirely different plant of tropical origin.
Cultural Information: Sweet potatoes are very sensitive to cold, and should not be planted until about a month after the date of the last frost. However, you should prepare the soil well before that. Sweet potatoes yield big crops with little effort when you start with healthy, well-rooted plants available from garden centers and through mail order catalogues. Buy only plants that are certified disease-free by the state Agricultural Department. Plants are made by cutting a sweet potato into sections or "slips," each containing an eye. (Don't use a sweet potato from a grocery store for planting because it has been treated to keep the eyes from sprouting.) An average sweet potato will provide between 6 and 8 slips. Start slips indoors in moist sand or vermiculite 8 to 10 weeks before the last frost date in your area. During this time they will grow a twelve-inch sprout. Cut the sprout back to two inches and plant the section in a good potting medium, where it will send down roots in approximately ten days to two weeks. It is now ready to transplant into the garden.

Work the soil to 6 or 8 inches deep. Space rows 3 feet apart. Lay out a furrow 3 to 4 inches deep and place an inch or two of compost in the bottom. Use fertilizer sparingly; a slow-release formula like 2–8–10 with low nitrogen is best (too much nitrogen will produce lush top growth but few tubers). Next, build a mound of soil up over the ridge to a height of about 10 inches, to allow easy harvesting later on. About two weeks or a month after the last frost, set the plants out. Push the plants 4 or 5 inches deep in the mound, but do not cover the bud. Place them 12 inches apart and water them well.

Mulch to keep out weeds and to hold the moisture. Growth cracks in the tubers are caused by moisture fluctuations in the soil. Sweet potatoes require 120 frost-free days to full maturity. They are subject to very few pest and disease problems.
Harvest: Dig the tubers on a dry bright day after the first light frost, or before frost blackens tips of the foliage. Dig very carefully and deeply under each plant, using a spading fork or shovel. The tubers bruise easily and will not keep well if injured. When the soil around the tubers has been loosened,

Sweet potatoes 'Bush Porto Rico' (copper-colored) and 'Centennial' (lighter orange)

go through the trenches with bare hands and lift the tubers carefully, gently spreading the tubers out in a semishady place to dry for a few hours.

Gently place sweet potatoes in ventilated crates or baskets. Bring the tubers indoors to cure. Store near the furnace or wherever you can maintain warm temperatures (about 80 degrees Fahrenheit), and where ventilation is adequate to draw away any humidity produced by the tubers. Allow them to dry under these conditions for 8 to 10 days. This helps heal any cuts or bruises, and toughens the sweet potato skins.

Then move tubers to a cooler location and store at 55 to 60 degrees Fahrenheit. Sweet potatoes can be harmed by storage temperatures lower than 50 degrees. Handle sweet potatoes as little as possible. Check stored tubers frequently, and discard any that show shriveling or decay.

Swiss Chard (Spinach Beet)
Goosefoot Family Easy ○
Days to Harvest: 45 to 55
Days to Germinate: 3 to 14
Temperature to Germinate: 68 to 86
Growth Temperature: 70 to 80 degrees Fahrenheit

Opposite, from top:
Winter squash 'Butter Boy Hybrid'
Squash 'Early Acorn Hybrid'
Summer squash from top left: pattypan, summer squash, crookneck, and zucchini

Height: 10 to 12 inches

Characteristics: For the home gardener, Swiss chard is one of the easiest-to-grow vegetables. Swiss chard is actually a bottomless beet, but it doesn't grow roots like beets. These beautiful plants produce dark-green leaves continuously during spring, summer, and fall and withstand hard frost. The leaves taste like a mild spinach. Burpee's 'Fordhook Giant' and Burpee's 'Rhubarb Chard' have succulent, crumpled leaves and thick, edible stalks that can be prepared like asparagus. 'Perpetual' has very little midrib and smaller, smoother leaves. (See "Planting Guide for Leafy Greens," page 42.)

The leaves can be used raw in salads or cooked as greens. They can also be substituted for spinach in your favorite recipes.

Burpee's 'Rhubarb Chard' with its dark green, crumpled leaves and bright crimson midribs and veins, is beautiful. Try planting it in your flower garden or as a pretty accent in a sunny shrub border. The plants are so prolific you need only a half dozen to supply a family of four for the summer.

Cultural Information: Swiss chard likes a pH of 6.0 to 6.8. Sow seeds in spring, planting in rows 15 inches wide, scattering the seeds an inch or so apart. Thin to 5 to 8 inches apart and eat the thinnings. The plants are adaptable to strong summer heat and cool summer nights. From time to time, check for aphids.

Harvest: You can harvest the leaves at any time, or harvest the first plants when they are about 6 inches high, cutting the entire plant to 1 inch above ground; the same plant will provide three or four harvests. Harvest only a few feet of the row at a time, and by the time you cut your way through the taller plants, the plants you harvested first will be ready to cut back again. Harvest continues until frost.

Tomatoes Nightshade Family Easy ○

Days to Harvest: 55 to 90*, depending on variety
Days to Germinate: 5 to 14
Temperature to Germinate: 68 to 86 degrees Fahrenheit
Growth Temperature: 75 to 80 degrees Fahrenheit
Height: 14 inches to 6 feet
Characteristics: Tomatoes are the number-one home-garden vegetable in America. In the Burpee catalog alone, there are more than thirty choices to suit every taste and fulfill every need. You can grow big brag-patch tomatoes, paste tomatoes for sauces, cherry or pear tomatoes, sweet, less-acid-tasting red, orange or yellow tomatoes, and even a winter-storage type like the 'Long-Keeper'. Many are disease-resistant. Many varieties bear some or all of these initials on their labels or seed packs: V.F.N.T. They indicate that the variety is tolerant to (V) Verticillium wilt, (F) Fusarium wilt, (N) Nematodes, and (T) Tobacco Mosaic Virus.

Tomato plants are either "indeterminate" or "determinate." Indeterminate types continue to bear fruit until frost kills them, often reaching a height of 6 feet or more, whether they are staked or caged. Most large-fruited, late-maturing varieties are indeterminate.

Determinate types stop growing when fruit has set on the terminal (growing) end. The plants are compact, and fruits ripen almost all at one time. In short-season areas or for large-scale home canning, this is an advantage. It's best not to prune or stake determinate types, but they do well in cages 2 to 4 feet tall.

Many gardeners plant early, midseason, and late varieties at one time so that the three varieties ripen in succession and extend the supply of fresh tomatoes throughout the season, right up to the fall frost. Burpee's 'Supersteak Hybrid VFN' is for tomato lovers who want a "beefsteak" tomato with full flavor and super size; most of the fruits weigh one to two pounds. 'Gardener's Delight' is our favorite cherry tomato and Burpee's 'VF Hybrid' is our favorite main-crop variety of medium large, rich red fruits. 'Roma VF' is recommended for its plum-shaped fruits with meaty interiors, excellent for sauces, catsup, and tomato paste.

Cultural Information: Tomatoes require full sun, at least 6 to 8 hours per day, for best production and growth. Select a sunny location where water does not stand after a heavy rain and where tomatoes, peppers, eggplants, or potatoes have not been grown for a year or longer.

If possible, start preparing your garden in the fall. Tomatoes prefer a pH balance of 5.5 to 6.5. (If necessary, add lime

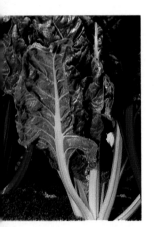

Above: Swiss chard 'Burpee's Rhubarb Chard' and 'Burpee's FORDHOOK® Giant' Below: Tomato 'Burpee's BIG BOY® Hybrid'

or sulfur to correct the pH. Work these in and let the garden stand over the winter.)

Start tomato seeds indoors 6 to 8 weeks before the last expected frost in your area. When transplanting to the garden, space plants 1½ to 2½ feet apart in all directions if plants are to be staked. If unsupported, space them 3 to 4 feet apart. It's best to check seed packs for specific distances for each variety. Keep plants well-watered during the growing season, especially during dry spells.

Keep weeds under control during the growing season. Mulch materials such as straw, grass clippings, papers, or black plastic help to retain soil moisture and maintain even soil temperature.

Unsupported plants will sprawl on the ground, require no pruning, and will probably produce a larger yield of smaller fruit than will staked plants. For larger, cleaner, more perfect fruits, support plants as they grow. Plants may be supported by stakes, cages, or trellises. See pages 34 and 39 for directions. *Harvest:* For optimal flavor and nutrition, leave tomatoes on the vine until completely ripe. To harvest, pull the fruit gently off the vine being careful not to bruise it, by holding the vine in one hand and pulling the fruit with the other.

Red-fruited varieties are ready to harvest when they are a full, deep red. Yellow- and orange-fruited varieties are fully ripe when their color is well developed and the calyx (stem top) is slightly dry. Burpee's winter storage tomato, 'Long-Keeper', has a light golden-orange skin

and medium-red flesh when ripe. Pick at this stage, or at the green-orange stage, to store for winter salads. Store 'Long-Keeper' fruits at room temperature and do not wrap.

In fall, protect plants from light frost by covering them with sheets, garden blankets, or plastic bags at night. When heavy frost is predicted, harvest all tomatoes, even those at the green-white stage. Allow them to ripen at room temperature or slightly cooler. Wrap them individually in tissue or newspaper. Carefully place them in single layers in shallow boxes, stem side down. Check the ripening tomatoes frequently and remove any that have bad spots. Some home gardeners move tomato plants in containers indoors so as to enjoy home-grown tomatoes for Thanksgiving dinner. 'Long-Keeper' tomatoes can be stored even longer—up until February and March—for salad additions all winter long.

Turnips Parsley Family Easy ○

Days to Harvest: 35 to 70, depending on variety
Days to Germinate: 3 to 7
Temperature to Germinate: 68 to 86 degrees Fahrenheit
Growth Temperature: 70 to 80 degrees Fahrenheit
Height: 10 to 12 inches
Characteristics: Turnips, with their delicate, slightly pungent flavor and crisp flesh, are an easy, relatively problem-free, quick-maturing crop that are tasty raw or cooked. 'Purple-Top White Globe' has mild flavor and is a beautiful root, with a round, smooth, bright

purplish-red top and creamy white bottom; it stores well. 'Tokyo Cross Hybrid' is an early variety, harvested in 35 days when the roots are 2 inches across. *Cultural Information:* Turnips grow best during cool weather in average, well-tilled (not too stony) soil supplemented with lime and potash—pH 5.5 to 7.0. They need a constant supply of water for high-quality roots. Sow any variety in late summer for fall use or winter storage. Plant in wide rows about 16 inches across and plant thickly. When plants are 4 to 5 inches tall, start thinning by hand (you can boil up the tasty young greens). Turnips are delicious raw and cooked. Frost improves flavor. To save space, turnips can be broadcast between rows of corn. Turnips have few pest or disease problems, but fleabeetles can be a problem in early spring. *Harvest:* The roots should be 2 to 4 inches in diameter, depending on the variety. They can be left in the ground for harvest during the winter.

Turnip, Canadian; see **Ru-tabaga**

Top: Plum tomatoes 'Roma VF'
Above: Tomato 'Cherry Grand Hybrid'
Below: Turnip 'Purple-Top White Globe'

Watercress

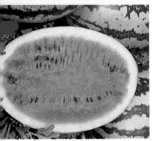

Below: Watermelon
'Yellow Baby Hybrid'
Bottom: Watermelon
'Sweet Favorite Hybrid'

Turnip, swedish; see *Rutabaga*

Turnip, yellow; see *Rutabaga*

Watercress Mustard Family Easy ◐ ○
Days to Harvest: 60 to 70
Days to Germinate: 4 to 14
Temperature to Germinate: 68 to 86 degrees Fahrenheit
Growth Temperature: 60 to 70 degrees Fahrenheit
Height: 3 to 6 inches
Characteristics: Oval, dark green, mildly pungent, peppery leaves for salads and garnishing. Watercress is a delicacy, very popular and delicious in sandwiches, soups, salads, and as a garnish.
Cultural Information: Watercress, as you might guess from the name, thrives where springs emerge from the ground or in small streams, and preferably in partial shade. Sow in small, clay pots set in a pan of water and later transplant to an outside location after the harsh spring frosts are over. Plant 6 to 8 inches apart. Water often to assure growth. The plants are hardy perennials and will live for years. Pinch back when about 6 inches high to encour-

age branching. Watercress is virtually pest-free. (See "Planting Guide for Leafy Greens," page 42.)
Harvest: Harvest when the leaves are enlarged. Plants can be started from cuttings. Watercress is especially tasty in the spring before flowers form (it is best not to let flowers develop; pinch them).

Watermelon Gourd Family Easy ○
Days to Harvest: 70 to 80
Days to Germinate: 4 to 14
Temperature to Germinate: 68 to 86 degrees Fahrenheit
Growth Temperature: 75 to 80 degrees Fahrenheit
Characteristics: Watermelons have either red or yellow flesh, and while most varieties have seeds, seedless varieties are available. Seedless varieties must be pollinated by standard varieties to provide proper fruiting. When gardeners order seedless varieties, Burpee always includes free seeds of a standard variety and recommends planting one hill of standard for every two or three hills of seedless. 'Fordhook® Hybrid' is an early variety, 74 days with 12- to 14-pound, nearly round watermelons. Burpee's 'Sugar Bush' takes only 80 days to produce 2 to 4 slightly oval "icebox"-type melons weighing 6 to 8 pounds each. 'Yellow Baby Hybrid' is unusual with its yellow flesh and small (under 10 pounds), oval melons.
Cultural Information: Some watermelons require a lot of growing space, but if your garden is small, there are varieties with short vines and a bush habit. Watermelons require more heat

than cantaloupes during the growing season, but gardeners who grow other melons successfully find they have good results with the smaller "icebox" varieties which mature earlier than other types. "Icebox" watermelons are round and weigh about 10 pounds. Other varieties are long or oval and usually weigh more than 20 pounds.

Plant in rich, well-drained soil with a pH of 6.2 to 6.8. Plant in hills placed 3 feet apart in rows 8 feet apart for vine types, as melons need lots of room to mature. Bush types can be spaced 2½ feet apart in rows 3 feet apart. Plastic mulch will help conserve moisture during dry periods. "Side-dress" with liquid fertilizer when fruit starts to form.

In areas where the growing season is short, watermelons may produce less sugar than those grown longer and may not be as sweet as you would expect. Choosing early-maturing varieties, starting seeds indoors and using plastic mulch to warm the soil early in spring all help compensate for a short growing season.

Watermelon is a vine crop and has the same pest and disease problems as the cucumber. (See "Planting Guide for Vine Crops," page 55.)
Harvesting: Judging when a watermelon is ripe is difficult. Prior to World War II, grocers used to "plug" them before their customers would buy them, and if they weren't properly ripe inside, the grocer was stuck with the unripe watermelon.

You can check the spot where the watermelon rests on the ground. It turns light green or yellow as the fruit reaches maturity. Also check the curly tendril on the leaf nearest the fruit; this commonly dries up when the melon is ripe. Examine the skin, which tends to become rough when the fruit is ready. Tap the melon with your knuckles. A dull sound indicates the melon is mature. Do your tapping in the morning, because later in the day the heat causes all melons to give a dull sound when rapped. Overripe melons also give off a dull sound when tapped, too, so you can see this is not a foolproof test.

To get the best flavor from watermelons, eat them chilled, but not ice-cold. They can be stored for weeks in a cool, dry place. And if you don't pickle the rinds, add them to your compost pile.

Planting in Hills

Planting "in hills" is a term for the method of planting seeds in clusters; these clusters need not be planted literally in raised mounds to form hills. When they are planted in raised mounds, 4 to 6 inches high, the advantages are that the soil warms faster and drains better, and water that collects around the base encourages roots to feed more deeply. Pumpkins, squash, and other vine crops are commonly planted in hills. Once the seedlings are established, the hills are thinned so that only the sturdiest seedlings remain.

PESTS AND DISEASES

Healthy, nutritious soil grows healthy, nutritious plants. Composting, which saves garbage collection and eases the burden on landfills while improving garden soil, is the single most important factor in growing healthy vegetables. At Burpee we believe chemicals aren't needed (or wanted) in the home vegetable garden. Whether you take organic or chemical steps to control pests and diseases, you won't have all-perfect vegetables. It's worth remembering that beauty is only skin deep; it's what's inside that counts. Wonderful flavor, good nutrition, and freedom from chemicals are what we strive for at Burpee with our vegetables.

If a plant routinely needs chemical pesticides to grow in your garden, ask yourself: Do I really need this plant? The instant cure that chemical pesticides seem to provide isn't without drawbacks. Make sure you understand chemical side effects before you use chemical pesticides. They stay in the soil and can seep in deep enough to contaminate drinking water. When sprayed on plants they kill beneficial and harmful insects and bacteria alike. Working with Mother Nature is easier, safer, healthier, and environmentally sound.

Use garden netting or row covers to keep larger insects off crops. There are biodegradable products (made by Safer, Inc. and Ringers) that replace the petrochemical insecticide, fungicide, and miticide products. For general advice and help with severe problems, it is always best to consult your local county extension service, which is up-to-date on the latest controls in your area.

Netting is a very effective deterent to flying insects and birds.

Five steps to a healthier, more productive garden:

1. Yearly replenish your soil with compost.
2. Most serious insect pest and disease problems can be avoided by crop rotation.
3. Learn which insects are beneficial. Invite them to stay in your garden by providing them with conditions they like.
4. Use soaker hoses or drip irrigation for watering. Overhead watering encourages fungus diseases.
5. Choose the right plant for the right place. If you notice one variety is very susceptible to disease, switch varieties. With so many choices, this shouldn't be a problem, in the limited space of a home vegetable garden.

KEEP THE GARDEN CLEAN

One of the best ways to avoid disease and pests in the garden is to keep the garden area clean. The best way to do this is to save a few minutes near the end of your garden chores to pick up any accumulated debris. Never let debris spend the week, or even the night, in your garden if you can help it. Bricks, wood, logs, glass, rotting weeds, and plants dying after the harvest are all invitations to pests, especially insects, slugs, and mice. Don't give them a home.

Check your plants regularly, especially the undersides of leaves, for any signs of pests. If a plant becomes heavily infested or diseased, be brutal: Uproot it and destroy it. Don't add it to your compost pile.)

When you harvest the tops of vegetables, dig up the roots, cut them up and add to your compost. And, when you harvest such root vegetables as potatoes, throw the stems and leaves on the compost pile. Don't let them rot in your garden.

Dig weeds up early, as soon as they show their little faces. This should include the entire garden site, even a section not currently in use. Halt the weeds early, using a hoe. They will be easy to control at this stage and once the tops are cut they will not grow back.

PESTS

It is unlikely that you will see more than one or two of these problems on your crops, but here is a list of the most frequent growing problems.

Aphids

These small, pear-shaped, sucking insects, often greenish-white, red or black (but sometimes taking on the color of the plant) gather on the most tender plant parts (usually, on new growth and the underside of leaves). There they suck plant sap, causing foliage to wither and a general loss of vigor.

They are from barely visible to ⅙ inch long. You will not have much trouble seeing them, since they enjoy family picnics, attaching to and damaging a plant in groups.

Aphids can carry disease. Worse, they secrete a sweet, sticky substance called "honey dew" which attracts ants and promotes the growth of a fungus known as "black sooty mold." This mold interferes with leaf function, slowing photosynthesis, and reduces the plant's vigor and yield.

Solutions: Sometimes a fairly strong spray from a hose on the underside of leaves will eliminate these pests. Control with Safer's® Insecticidal Soap with a natural—and biodegradable—insecticide formula. Introduce aphids' natural enemies, including ladybugs, lacewings, and parasitic wasps. All are available by mail order from Burpee and other garden supply catalogs. Mechanical controls can be useful too. Plants known to repel aphids are pennyroyal, spearmint, and tansy.

Beetles

There are many different kinds of beetles (Mexican Bean Beetle, Japanese Beetle, Flea beetle, Colorado Potato Beetle, Cucumber Beetle) that, depending on which part of the country you live in and what vegetables you grow, might appear in your garden. Serious beetle infestations are relatively rare. It is also very difficult for a home gardener to positively identify some beetles without visiting the garden at night with a flashlight and a magnifying hand lens. The most common are mentioned here and the solutions are similar.

The **Colorado beetles** are especially harmful at the larval stage. Larvae are plump, reddish-orange, soft-bodied insects with dark heads and black markings. Adults are large beetles with yellow and black stripes. Colorado beetles aren't confined to

Natural Solutions for Fighting Pests and Diseases

Mother Nature, in her system of checks and balances, has provided us with many plants that can be used as sources of insecticides and bacterial agents for fighting harmful insects.

Bacillus thuringiensis (Bt): It is sold under the trade names of Ringer Attack® and "Thuricide." When eaten by caterpillars, it paralyzes their digestive system; it doesn't harm birds, bees, pets, or humans.

Bacillus popilliae or Milky Spore: Ringer™ Grub Attack. It kills by infecting grubs with Milky Spore disease, caused by bacillus popilliae. Infected grubs stop feeding and die, releasing billions of new spores to kill other grubs. A single application provides ten or more years of control.

1% Rotenone: It is effective right up to harvest without danger of harmful residues. Made from roots and stems of tropical vines, it acts as a stomach poison for many sucking and chewing insects.

Insecticidal soaps: Biodegradable insecticides in liquid soap concentrate are safe and effective. Safer's has a line of soaps for different purposes.

Aphid

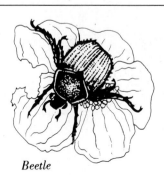

Beetle

Colorado; they can be found wherever potatoes or eggplant are grown.

There are two types of **Cucumber Beetles:** the **spotted cucumber beetle** and the **striped cucumber beetle.** The first, about ¼ inch long, has black spots on greenish-yellow wings; the head is black. The striped cucumber beetle is somewhat smaller, and yellow with three black stripes on its back. Both spotted and striped cucumber beetles feed on leaves, flowers, and fruit of all vine crops, and when yellow-white larvae, they chew on roots too. They transmit bacterial wilt and mosaic virus. Radishes, summer savory and tansy repel these beetles.

The adults of the **Mexican Bean Beetles** are ¼-inch-long ovals. They are copper in color, with black dots on their backs. They feed on the leaves, stems, and pods of all kinds of bean plants. Potatoes, rosemary, and summer savory help repel them.

The **Japanese Beetle,** the bane of eastern United States gardeners, continues to move west. It has a voracious appetite, feeding on over 300 different plants, fruits, vegetables, and flowers.

Flea Beetles are small, black, quick-jumping beetles that chew small holes in foliage and can spread disease. Plants that repel them are head lettuce, mint, and wormwood.

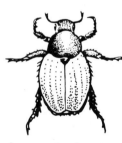

Japanese beetle

Solution: Handpick the beetles or the caterpillars off. Some beetles lay their eggs in the soil, others on the underside of leaves. Check the underside of leaves for eggs (Colorado Potato Beetles' are orange, laid in rows; Mexican Bean Beetles' are yellow) and squash them. Covering rows of plants early in the season with a garden blanket or nets will prevent the insects from laying their eggs on the leaves and the beetles from landing later. Cultivate soil around the plants to destroy eggs of the Flea Beetle. Diatomaceous earth spread around the plants can destroy the larvae. A thick layer of mulch will sometimes prevent hatching beetles from reaching plants. Bran cereal sprinkled on moist leaves will be ingested by beetles, causing internal swelling and death. Planting early allows the plants to become more vigorous and resistant before the beetles hatch. Try planting potatoes and bush beans in alternate rows; this seems to discourage the beetles. Finally, spray with Ringer's Colorado Potato Beetle Attack®. After ingesting sprayed foliage, the beetles stop eating and die in two to five days. The spray, made from natural ingredients, can be used right up to harvest.

Beetle traps which lure the insects to their deaths are available at garden stores and can be effective.

Cutworm

Cabbage Looper, Cabbage Worm

This brownish, nocturnal moth emerges in spring. It lays eggs in the soil, where they will overwinter to hatch into worms.

Solution: Keep young plants covered with garden blankets to prevent moths from laying their eggs. Handpick and destroy them. Sprinkle plants with wood ashes or salt. *Bacillus thuringiensis* (Bt) is effective and readily available at garden centers for a natural solution.

Cutworms

Smooth, fat, and 2 inches in length, ranging in color from brown and black to gray. They feed at night, often cutting newly set plants off at ground level.

Solution: Cut a collar from a paper cup and set it around the base of each plant when transplanting to the garden. An empty tin cup with the bottom removed makes another good collar. Wood ashes tilled into soil in autumn or early spring will keep cutworms away, because they don't like to crawl through rough soil.

Leafhoppers

Tiny (1/8-inch) insects, pale-green with white spots. They hop about, chewing leaves and stems, stunting growth; may also spread disease as they feed.

Solution: Keep plants covered with garden blankets. Keep your garden free of debris, a favorite leafhopper nesting spot. Safer's® Insecticidal Soap is often helpful.

Mites

Tiny yellow, green, red or brown insects, usually found on the undersides of leaves, they are barely visible to the naked eye. Their webs may be visible, giving infected plants a "dusty" appearance. They stunt plant growth.

Solution: Apply Safer's® Insecticidal Soap, the only effective control today. Dust infected plants with lime. Mites tend to be a worse problem in hot, dry weather.

Nematodes

While nematodes are not true insects, we've placed them here for simplicity's sake. These tiny worms, microscopic in size, attach to plant roots, causing swellings (galls) to form. Plants may wilt or appear stunted. Nematodes are a serious problem in many southern areas.

Solution: Have the soil tested for nematodes through the county extension office before planting. Do not plant in infested soils. To combat nematodes, plant marigolds. Interplant your vegetables with French marigolds, especially *T. signata pumula*. These will grow for the entire season, making your vegetable garden picturesque, giving you flowers for cutting. Rotate your

crops, and keep your garden clean and free of weeds and refuse.

Plant nematode-resistant vegetables when possible. Nematode-resistant plants include: Broccoli, Brussels Sprouts, Mustard, Chives, Garlic, Leek, Rutabaga, Turnip.

Squash Bugs

These mottled light-and-dark-brown insects are flat and wide, usually about ½ inch long. Squash bugs give off a peculiar, pungent odor when they are crushed. As they feed, they inject a toxic substance into the plant, causing a condition that resembles bacterial wilt. Affected vines turn black and crisp, and younger plants may be killed. Squash bugs can be found in colonies on unripe fruits and on stems and leaves of vines. They lay shiny, brick-red eggs on the undersides of leaves when the plants begin to vine.

Solution: Trap adult bugs by placing boards on the soil around your vine crops. The bugs will seek the moisture and shade under the boards, and can be crushed there. The bugs can be hand-picked from the plants, the eggs scraped off the leaves. A natural enemy of the squash bug is the tachinid fly. Try sowing radish seeds in the hills with squash or cucumbers; they are known to repel squash bugs. Nasturtiums and tansy planted nearby will also help.

Stink Bugs

Found mostly in the South, they give off a terrible odor when crushed. Stink bugs puncture fruits to feed, causing hard, white spots to form inside fruits.

Solution: Keep weeds under control, as adults will winter-over in debris and can produce several generations each year.

Leafhopper

Tomato Hornworms

Large, bright-green caterpillars, "horned" at the rear end, which can quickly devour the foliage of tomatoes and other plants of the same family, including potatoes, eggplants, and peppers.

Solution: Handpick and destroy them. *Bacillus thuringiensis* (Bt) is a safe natural solution available in powdered or liquid form under the trade names of Dupel and Thuricide, among others.

Vine Borers

These are wrinkled, fat, white caterpillars with dark heads, about 1 inch long, hatched from eggs laid by a clear-winged moth. Vine borers tunnel their way into plant stems and remain there, feeding as they move along. Signs of borer infestation include small entry holes near the bases of stems, small piles of greenish, sawdust-like material on the ground near the holes, and sudden wilting of the vine.

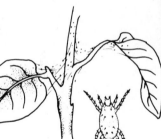

Spider mite

Solution: When you notice signs of borer infestation, use a knife to slit the stem away from the base until you find the borer, then pry it out and destroy it. If the stem is badly damaged or wilted, cut it off and destroy it. Do not add it to your compost pile, for there may be other borers in the same stem. If the stem does not seem to be substantially weakened, bend it down gently to ground level and cover it with soil so that rooting may occur. Remove all weeds from your garden to help prevent infestation, and dust your vine crops with rotenone when the plants begin to vine. An effective deterrent is to wrap aluminum foil around the bottom 4 to 5 inches of the plant before it blooms, then sprinkle black pepper on the soil around the base of the plant. The pepper repels the egg-laying moths, and reflection from the foil confuses them.

Whitefly

Small, white flying insects that rise up in a cloud when plants are brushed. They suck sap from leaves, leaving a sticky substance. Leaves tend to brown and fall off.

Solution: Very difficult pest to control, both outdoors and in the greenhouse. Outdoors, your friend the green lacewing can eat up lots of whitefly for you. Safer's® Insecticidal Soap may help limit the whitefly population. Whitefly is attracted to bright yellow. To make your own whitefly trap, coat a piece of yellow cardboard with a sticky substance like honey or motor oil and tuck it in the pot. Nasturtiums planted nearby help repel whitefly.

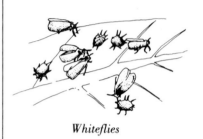

Whiteflies

DISEASES

Anthracnose

This is a fungus disease which first appears as yellowish, decaying spots on leaves. The spots enlarge quickly, then turn brown and fall out, leaving large, ragged holes. Long, dark spots with lighter-colored centers develop on stems. Young fruit may be killed, and larger fruit sometimes develop sunken cankers that ooze. Anthracnose is most often carried by diseased plant refuse and spread by splashing water. It thrives in humid weather or during extended periods of rain.

Solution: Control by rotating crops, keeping fruits off the ground by staking or using cages, and by treating plants with a fungicide. Remove infected foliage and fruit.

Powdery Mildew

You'll notice a dirty-white substance covering the plant when powdery mildew is present. Leaves dry out and curl, buds die before blooming. Some vegetables like zucchini develop mildew at the end of their growing season, when it is no longer worth worrying about.

Prevention: Give your plants fresh air by spacing them as prescribed on the seed packet. Good air circulation will help to avoid the damp conditions mildew needs to flourish. Don't use overhead watering, especially late in the day, when water on the foliage does not have a chance to dry.

Wilt

Wilt can be caused by three different factors. It can be a physiological problem, a simple lack of water in the soil; it can be a pathological problem, caused by fungi plugging up the water-conducting tissue in the roots and stems of the plants; and it can be bacterial wilt, also called Stewart's Disease wherein, unlike most wilts, the vines wilt gradually and die without any yellowing of the foliage. The symptoms are the same, a droopy plant with downward-curling leaves.

Lack of water causes the plant to droop because the water channels in the leaves and the stem just quit working and become limp. The plant will recover and regain its stiffness when watered, unless it has been dry too long. To avoid this problem, water your plants regularly and deeply, and fertilize them to promote vigorous growth.

When the problem is a fungus disease called wilt, the plants can't recover, even when watered, because the water-conducting tubes are plugged up with the fungus organism.

One way to check for bacterial wilt in your vine crops is to slice a stem and look for a white, sticky, stringy substance. Bacterial wilt is spread by cucumber beetles and flea beetles, so it is important to keep the insects under control. Rotate plant crops. Infected plants must be removed and destroyed.

Prevention: When buying seeds or plants, choose the varieties that are wilt-resistant. Happily, acorn and butternut squash both seem to be resistant to bacterial wilt. "Wilt-resistant" means resistant to the fungus disease, but no plant is resistant to being too dry, so provide proper watering. Most wilt disease is soil-borne and, by rotating crops and building a healthy soil by adding compost, it can be prevented.

ANIMALS IN THE GARDEN

Animals in the vegetable garden are usually more a problem for rural gardeners, but they can bother city dwellers too. The most effective defense is a good fence. The height and the depth depend on the animal pests in your area. It is better to recognize this need early in the gardening season, when you can prevent problems, then to try and save the expense and be sorry later. There are many inexpensive fencing materials, chicken wire for example, that are effective. You want your garden to be as successful as possible; discouraged or disappointed gardeners miss out on all the fun.

Birds

For the most part, birds are our friends, eating aphids, beetles, and harmful caterpillars. But sometimes they go too far, eating our lunch.

There are many different sizes of nylon netting that can be draped over plants to protect them. The netting can be reused for many years, if dried and gently folded before storing.

There are plastic snakes, owls, or even scarecrows that can be put in your garden to frighten the birds away; it is necessary for you to periodically move them from spot to spot. If they are not moved, the birds will wise up and be sitting on the scarecrow's shoulder in no time. To protect corn, some gardeners slip paper bags over the ripening ears.

Deer

They can devastate entire crops and will do considerable damage to the garden. The only way to safely control them is to fence in your garden with an 8-foot fence. For added protection, string along the top of your fence an electric wire, the kind used to fence in livestock. The wire will give any adventuresome deer a slight shock, which will discourage them from returning.

Most of the recommendations we have found to be effective are not very pretty for your garden. For example, hanging a bar of soap (gardeners differ on the brands they recommend, and the brand should probably be changed from time to time anyway) several places throughout the garden.

The problem is that what works in one area doesn't necessarily work in another, and what worked for one week doesn't continue to work indefinitely. Deer, if hungry enough, will really try your patience.

Hang kerosine or creosote-soaked rags, or perforated cans of mothballs (napthalene) around the edge of the garden. That can keep deer out for a short period. Rags should be re-treated at monthly intervals.

Commercial deer repellents are available. Be sure to read the directions carefully. Some

of these spray shouldn't be used on or near plants grown for food. An electric fence—high enough so that deer can't jump over it—will be effective. If you are experiencing very serious damage, contact your local county agricultural agent. This may indicate a widespread deer-management problem, and he may have experience that can help you.

Dogs and Cats

Dogs and cats can be a nuisance (especially if they belong to someone else). They love to dig and leave their droppings in freshly prepared or loose soil. In other words, they like perfect garden conditions.

A fence or wire mesh around the garden area could keep them out. Protect seed beds by laying chicken wire on the soil. Remove wire before the plants become too large to slip through the mesh.

Sometimes, a well-directed dousing with a hose might discourage them from wandering into your garden.

Groundhogs and Woodchucks

They eat your choicest vegetables and can cause enormous damage in just one night. They burrow and leave holes and piles of dirt. If only we could harness and train them for tilling!

Leave Havahart™ animal traps to catch them; then, you can remove them to another area.

NOTE: Always wear gloves and protective clothing when handling wild animals as they may be diseased.

You can try to fence them out with wire fence 3 feet high. Bend the bottom 12 inches away from the garden and bury it a few inches deep in the soil. Leave the upper 18 inches of fence unattached to the supporting stakes and bend this portion outward. The weight of the animal as he climbs will pull the upper portion down towards the ground. Or, make a fence 6 feet tall, buried at least 6 inches into the soil.

Mice, Moles, Voles, and Gophers

They eat exposed parts of vegetables and make runways and nests in tall grass. Mole and mouse traps will help control the problem.

A fence made of ¼-inch mesh wire 12 inches high and extended 12 inches below the soil surface to prevent tunneling underneath will keep them out. Consider mowing areas of tall grass near vegetable gardens. These pests try to find their food as close to home as possible, and if they have no place near your garden to nest, most likely they won't come for a visit.

When you control moles' food supply, you control mole populations. Moles love grubs; follow the directions on page 81 to rid your garden of beetle larvae and grubs.

Rabbits

They love to steal the vegetables from your garden in spring, summer, and fall.

Enclose the garden with a fence of 1-inch chicken wire, 30 inches high. It should last for several years.

Use a Havahart™ animal trap and release the rabbits in a rural area. Unfortunately, because these traps are baited, they work better in the winter; the rabbits will probably prefer to continue eating your garden lettuce during the growing season.

Spread pepper around the plants they like to eat. They sniff a lot and the pepper will repel them. Commercial rabbit repellents are available too.

Raccoons

Their favorite trick is to rob your corn at night, right at the early maturity stage. Again, the Havahart™ trap is one option.

A 4-foot-high fence, with the top extending 18 inches above the post supports, should help. As the raccoon climbs up on the unattached portion, his weight will pull the fence down to the ground.

You might try a low-voltage electric fence. Use lightweight wire fed by a battery-operated charger; place two wires on the insulators, one wire 4 to 6 inches above the ground and a second wire 4 to 6 inches higher. Keep the ground clear under the wires so no weeds short the circuit current.

You can sprinkle corn silks with red pepper, but you'll have to repeat it whenever it rains. Finally, try draping work clothes around the garden, or leave a portable radio playing overnight.

Rats

Rats are sneaky and hard to see. They do more damage than is usually realized and we tend to attribute it to other pests. Because rats carry disease, every effort to control or eliminate this pest should be made.

Keep the garden area cleaned up. Remove old and rotted vegetables, and keep them in a compost bin that can't become a breeding and hiding area for pests.

Use steel-snap traps or poison baits. These must be used with great care (so that children and pets aren't endangered), checked, and removed when necessary. Follow the manufacturer's directions.

The ladies in Burpee's customer service department answering mail at the turn of the century.

GARDENERS' MOST-ASKED QUESTIONS

The first Burpee catalog was mailed in 1876, and the catalogs have been coming ever since, offering gardeners a wealth of seeds, plants, fruits, shrubs, and trees, as well as advice for better gardening. From the earliest years, Burpee has received letters from custom-ers describing their gardens and asking questions. Today our "Gardening Hot Line" receives over thirty-five thousand phone calls a year. Here are the most frequently asked questions about vegetables.

GETTING STARTED

Q: What can I plant for fall crops?
A: This depends on your first expected frost date. Areas with a first frost around November 10 can sow lettuce, onions, parsley, garden peas, radish, and spinach. Areas that don't get frost until November 30 through December can sow most crops. We suggest you order seeds for fall sowing along with your regular spring order, to ensure you have the varieties you want when you need them.

Q: Are there any vegetables that will tolerate shade?
A: Nearly all vegetables require 6 to 8 hours of sunlight every day. The only vegetables that will tolerate growing in a partially shady location are the salad crops, such as lettuce and other leafy greens.

GROWING FROM SEED

Q: My seed order was left overnight in freezing temperatures. Will this harm the seed?
A: Overnight freezing temperatures should not be injurious to your seeds, provided the seed package was kept dry.

Q: I have seed left from last year. Will they still grow?
A: Most seed left over from the previous year will give partial germination the following year. Seed packets should be stored in a cool, moderately dry atmosphere. Some kinds of seed, including lettuce, parsnip, and parsley, will not stay viable. For best results, always use fresh seed.

Q: My seedlings are always pale and spindly-looking. What did I do wrong?
A: Tall, pale, spindly seedlings are the result of overcrowding or insufficient light. As soon as seedlings develop two pairs of true leaves, they should be transplanted, spaced to stand at least 2 inches apart. See pages 23–25 for more information.

Q: There is mold growing on my Seed'n Starts®. Will it hurt the plants?
A: Mold growing on Seed'n Starts® can cause damping off, destroying the seed before it emerges or killing the seedlings.

The Seed'n Starts® are being watered too often or are kept too wet during cloudy weather. If the seedlings are up, make sure they get good ventilation (but do not place in a draft) and good light.

Q: How do I store my potato eyes until I can plant them?
A: Potatoes and onions are shipped in vermiculite packing material, for insulation and moisture control. Keep the package intact in a cool (frost-free), dry, dark place until you are ready to plant. There is no need to open the package until you want to plant them.

GROWING

Q: Why won't my flowers bloom or vegetables set fruit? The plants appear very healthy.
A: Your garden soil probably has too much nitrogen, applied either in the form of fertilizer or fresh manure. Excessive nitrogen produces vegetative growth at the expense of the flower or fruit production. Do not fertilize indiscriminately. A soil test will reveal what type and quantities of fertilizer, lime, or other elements your ground may need.

Q: I purchased several packages of earthworms and now there is no trace of them. How can I get them to stay in my garden?
A: Work in compost, humus, decayed garbage and rotted newspapers. This gives worms something to eat and a reason to stay in your garden area.

Q: How long does it take asparagus to begin growth after planting? Mine has been in the ground one month.
A: Asparagus roots may take well over a month to become established and show shoots. If the soil is too heavy or planting is too deep, it could take longer.

Q: Why did my vine crop wilt and die early in the season?
A: Probably due to the disease known as bacterial wilt, where plants wilt and die without showing any yellow foliage. Slit a stem and look for a white, sticky, stringy substance, indicating the disease. It is important to keep insects under control as the disease is spread by cucumber beetles. Here we do recommend you spray with a natural insecticide, from the time the vine starts to develop until blossoms appear. Use rotenone.

Q: Why do cabbage and lettuce go to seed?
A: Premature bolting (going to seed) occurs when weather is too hot at the time plants are maturing. Give your plants plenty of room to grow, for good air circulation and light. Plant early enough so crop can develop before the hot weather sets in.

Q: The accessory roots seem thwarted when vine crops are grown on black plastic. Will the vines die if accessory roots don't actually root?
A: Plastic mulch is a natural for vine crops. Commercial growers find the benefits of producing clean, worm-free fruits far outnumber the need for secondary roots to take hold. Plants will not die if these roots don't develop. Planting the crop on slightly raised hills or beds will provide higher soil temperatures and better aeration. Black polyethylene mulch spread down the row will promote rapid growth by warming the soil 3 or 4 degrees Fahrenheit and eliminating weeds in the row.

Q: My vine crops are producing oddly shaped, oddly colored fruits!
A: Small, misshapen fruits may be the result of poor or incomplete pollination due to poor weather conditions, or may be a result of unintended cross-pollination. Plants of the same botanical species will readily cross-pollinate and produce off-types for color or shape. This is why it is important to plant fresh seed each year.

Q: My cucumbers produced very few fruits last season. How can I be assured of an abundant fruit set this year?
A: Cucumbers produce male and female flowers on separate plants. Male flowers often appear first, followed by female flowers that can be distinguished by tiny fruit buds at the base of the petals. Cucumbers depend on bees for pollination, which usually occurs during the morning when the bees are moving about, transferring pollen from blossom to blossom.

To make sure the first female flowers on the vine produce fruit, break off a newly opened male flower in the morning and rub the pollen-laden stamen (the spur in the center of the flower)

around the inside of the newly opened female flower.

Q: *The ends of my cucumbers and squash rot on the vine, and the muskmelon rots on the ground without ripening. Why?*
A: This sounds like blossom end rot, not caused by disease but by weather conditions—usually insufficient or uneven water supply. Controls include soaking soil thoroughly to a depth of 8 inches, avoiding heavy doses of nitrogen, not cultivating in dry weather, and mulching. The use of a mulch such as black plastic helps retain necessary moisture in the soil, and keeps the soil warm and free from the weeds that rob other plants of water. Bonus: Plastic mulch keeps the fruits clean, preventing them from resting on the earth where they can pick up disease and insects.

Q: *My cucumbers are bitter. Why?*
A: This can be caused by a genetic trait but is usually caused by extreme temperature fluctuations. It can also be due to the lack of certain soil nutrients, so you may want to test your soil if the problem persists.

Q: *My cucumbers are producing round fruit, some like golfballs, some the size of grapefruit. Why?*
A: Small or misshapen cucumber fruit is frequently caused by incomplete pollination. If bees are scarce or cool weather slows their activity, or if you spray and kill bees, you will have more misshapen fruits. To encourage more complete pollination, pick male blossoms and transfer the pollen to the female blossoms by rubbing the male anthers across the top of the female stigma.

Q: *My zucchini did not set fruits this year. Why not?*
A: This is probably due to the lack of or incomplete pollination, often caused by chemical spraying or lack of bee activity. If zucchini are planted too late in the season, they don't have time to cross-pollinate.

Q: *Why do my bush beans vine?*
A: Excess water and nitrogen make the central flower stem elongate in bush beans, thus giving them the appearance of pole beans. This is particularly noticeable in bush lima beans.

Q: *The leaves of my peas yellow and drop; the pods and seeds are immature. Why?*
A: Your peas are infected with a root rot. Fungus that causes root rot lives in soil, so crop rotation is important for control.

Q: *Why did seeds develop in my seedless watermelon?*
A: Stress conditions in the weather and soil composition can cause any seedless variety to develop seeds. Sometimes, too, when seedless varieties cross with regular varieties, you may get seeds in the resulting fruit.

Q: *What causes carrots to grow white?*
A: White or colorless carrots are usually the result of soil that lacks lime or is too rich in nitrogen. Carrots need plenty of water to grow well and prefer a well-lined, well-aerated, sandy soil. If soil is poor, an addition of slow-release 5–10–5 fertilizer will be helpful. Have your soil tested if poor results continue.

Q: *Why did my 'Tokyo Cross' turnip go to flower without producing any roots?*
A: The 'Tokyo Cross' hybrid turnip grows best if planted in the spring, while the weather is still cool. If planted later, the plants may bolt (go to seed prematurely) as the weather gets warmer, rather than producing roots. We suggest planting this variety earlier, thereby allowing plants time to develop good roots before the weather gets hot and forces plants to go to seed.

Q: *My radishes produce large top growth but no bulbs (radishes) at the bottom. What did I do wrong?*
A: Lack of bulb development is usually due to incorrect thinning. As soon as the seedlings produce their first pair of true leaves, thin the plants to no less than 1 inch apart.

Q: *What keeps my tomatoes from ripening on the top?*
A: Your tomatoes have "green shoulders," a perplexing problem caused by extreme environmental conditions, nutrient deficiencies, poor light, or virus. Try to maintain good cultural practice regarding feeding, watering, and pruning your plants.

Q: *Why did my tomato plants produce all vine and no fruit?*
A: This could be due to too-rich soil. Excessive fertilizer applications may result in ac-

celerated plant growth without fruit. If nitrogen is needed, apply after lots of fruit is set on the plant.

Q: What causes deformed, cat-faced tomatoes?
A: Large-fruited varieties have a large blossom end scar where the pistil abscesses. When there are low temperatures and wide fluctuations of available moisture, abnormal growth results.

Q: Why do tomato skins crack?
A: This often occurs after heavy rains or heavy irrigation, but humidity probably has more to do with it than anything else. 'Heinz 1350' is resistant to cracking.

Q: My potatoes were quite large this year but hollow in the center!
A: This is known as "hollow heart," and it usually develops due to excessive soil moisture and/or fertility. Plant in well-drained soils and space the plants a few inches closer together.

Q: My potato plants look like they are forming small tomatoes!
A: This is actually a seed pod forming on your potato plants. It turns red, giving the impression of a tomato. These pods are not edible; remove them from the plant, as formation of seed pods drains strength from the tubers, the reason for grow-

ing potatoes in the first place. Don't be tempted to save the pods for planting; rate of germination is very low.

Q: Why were there few ears and poor kernel development on my sweet corn?
A: (1) Corn is wind-pollinated, so short block plantings (such as a minimum of four rows of hills) is better for pollination than a single row; (2) If planted too close together or in partial shade, ears will not develop; (3) You must have proper soil moisture for ear development. The need for water is greater from tasseling to picking time. No check in water should occur during that period; 4) Have the soil tested for fertilizer needs; (5) Plant in a new section of the garden each year to prevent spreading any disease or insect problems; (6) If corn is lacking kernels near the end of the ear, this is probably due to rains washing off pollen, thus a lack of complete ear pollination.

Q: My cabbage and lettuce always go to seed before forming heads.
A: Your plants suffer from hot weather, which causes them to bolt (go to seed prematurely). For good head lettuce, sow seed early indoors. Transplant the seedlings into pots and harden off in a cold frame. Or, sow the seed in the garden, keeping plants in each row at least 15

inches apart. Good heads can't form unless the plants have plenty of room. For fall harvest, sow seed late July or early August.

Q: What is the blue-grey powdery stuff on top of my Brussels sprouts?
A: Your plants, infested with aphids, were probably covered with the sticky secretion "honeydew." Evidently some mold then formed on the honeydew. Control the aphids (see page 81) and the mold should go away.

Q: The upper halves of my spinach plants are turning brown and drying out. Why?
A: Two possible causes: (1) Tipburn: The outer edges or upper portion of the plant turns brown or dies back due to unfavorable weather in early spring. There is no known control; (2) Yellow Mosaic Virus: This virus, spread by aphids and leafhoppers, can be controlled by destroying nearby weeds that harbor these insects.

Q: My peppers are not setting fruit. Why?
A: Unfavorable temperatures and scant water supply are the basic factors in the dropping of buds, blossoms, and small fruit. Temperatures below 60 degrees Fahrenheit or above 75 degrees Fahrenheit at night discourage fruit set. Winds may also decrease fruit set.

HARVESTING

Q: *What causes onions to rot in storage?*

A: If you plan to grow onions for storage, select only those varieties recommended as good keepers. Onions must be thoroughly dry to keep well. Damaged, soft, or immature onions, those with thick necks, or seed stalks, and those grown from sets do not store well. ("Sets" are onions grown to the size of scallions, then shipped to the gardener for planting and growing outdoors.) Store in a dry, well-ventilated place, such as an unheated room or attic where the temperature can be kept around 30 to 40 degrees Fahrenheit. Do not store in cellars—too damp. Place onions in slatted crates or open-mesh bags. Fill the bags half-full and hang them on hooks. Fill crates half-full and stack them several inches off the floor.

Q: *I harvested my sunflowers, only to find the majority of the seeds were not fully developed. Why did this happen?*

A: Sunflowers have some particular needs. 1) They need warm, sunny weather to mature, and although they require plenty of moisture during the growing season, the soil must be well drained. 2) Sunflowers must be pollinated in order to set seed; this is usually accomplished by bees or wind. 3) The flower head must be harvested when fully mature. The spongy center of the green seed head dries slowly and should be almost a light brown by the time it's ready for harvest. Left on too long, it will shatter or birds will eat the seeds.

Q: *How do I harvest and cure Luffa gourds?*

A: Harvest before the first frost or when the shells begin to harden. Place the fruit in a tub or sink under running water and peel off the outer skin as you would peel an orange, exposing the inner sponge. Cleanse the sponge of juices and loose particles by repeatedly squeezing it in the water. When the sponge has dried, you can shake out the seeds.

Q: *When is winter squash ready to harvest?*

A: Winter squash is ready to harvest when it has turned a solid color and the rind has hardened. (When the spot touching the ground turns a yellowish-orange, such varieties as acorn squash are ready for harvest.) Be sure to harvest before hard frost strikes. Bruised or immature fruits will not store well and should be used quickly. Cut the fruit from the vine, leaving 2 inches of stem attached. After harvest, cure for a week or two at a temperature of 75 to 85 degrees Fahrenheit, to harden the shell, then store in a cool, dry place with a temperature range of 50 to 55 degrees Fahrenheit.

Burpee's Gardening Hot Line would be happy to answer your questions. Write or call:

W. Atlee Burpee & Company
300 Park Avenue
Warminster, PA 18974
215–674–9612

Please also write or call for a free Burpee catalog:

215–674–9633

THE USDA PLANT HARDINESS MAP OF THE UNITED STATES

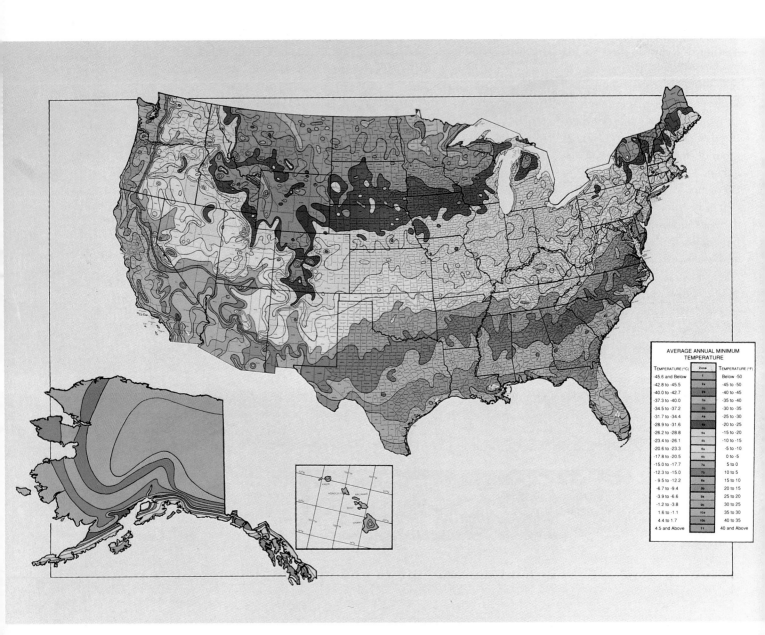

INDEX